HOW TO BE A LADY:

A

BOOK FOR GIRLS,

CONTAINING USEFUL HINTS ON THE FORMATION
OF CHARACTER.

D0684884

BY THE

REV. HARVEY NEWCOMB.

Crown Rights Book Company
www.crownrights.com

GLASGOW:

WILLIAM COLLINS, QUEEN'S PRINTER.

1862.

Reprinted 2008

Printed in Dixie.

For a catalogue listing of other available titles,
or for wholesale discounts, please contact:

Crown Rights Book Company
Post Office Box 386 Dahlonega, Georgia 30533

e-mail: books@crownrights.com
website: www.crownrights.com

PREFACE.

"PREFACE! I never read a preface, it's *so prosy*,"
said a bright-eyed, sprightly little girl: "I want to
get at the story." Her object in reading was *to be
amused*. If she had desired to be benefited by what
she read, she would have perused the Author's preface,
in order to understand why he wrote the book. The
Author, having daughters of his own, and having been
many years employed in writing for the young, hopes to
be able to offer some good advice, in the following pages,
in an entertaining way, for girls or misses, between the
ages of eight and fifteen. His object is, to assist them
in forming their characters upon the best model; that
they may become well-bred, intelligent, refined, and
good; and then they will be LADIES, in the highest
sense. The Illustrations are not mere collections of
stories, for the *amusement* of juvenile readers. Such, and
such only, have been selected as could be made to con-
vey some useful instruction to the mind, or produce
some good impression upon the heart. They have been
collected from a great variety of sources, some new and
some old; but in nearly every case entirely re-written,
and such reflections added as have seemed necessary,
to impress upon the mind of the reader the lessons
which they teach. It is probable that some of the

anecdotes may be already familiar. If so, they are here presented in a *new dress,* and made to serve a *new purpose;* so that they will bear another reading. It is believed, however, that most of them will be new to those into whose hands they may fall; and the Author hopes that they may prove both entertaining and useful to a class of young people, whose happiness and future usefulness he sincerely desires to promote.

This book covers substantially the same ground occupied by another work for boys, issued simultaneously with it. Some parts of both are identical; while other parts are entirely different. If it shall be the means of benefiting one immortal mind, the Author will be abundantly rewarded.

CONTENTS.

CHAPTER I.

CHAPTER II.

CHAPTER III.

CHAPTER IV.

CHAPTER V.

CHAPTER VI.

HOW TO BE A LADY.

CHAPTER I.

ON CHILDHOOD AND YOUTH.

IN one sense, very young persons are apt to think too much of themselves; in another, not enough. When they think they know more than their parents and teachers, or other elderly people, and so set up to be *bold* and *smart*, then they think too much of themselves. It used to be said, when I was a boy, that " Young folks *think* old folks are fools; but old folks *know* young folks are fools." Although I would be very far indeed from calling you *fools*, because you have already acquired much knowledge, and have the capacity for acquiring much more, yet, with reference to such knowledge as is acquired by *experience*, and in comparison with *what there is to be known*, there is " more truth than *poetry*," in the old adage. But, when young people suppose it is of no consequence what they do, or how they behave, *because they are young*, then they do not think enough of themselves.

Should you see a man riding with a little stick for a whip, you would not think his stick worth your notice at all; but the biggest tree that ever I saw, grew from a little willow stick that a man rode home with, and then planted in his garden. You have sat under the beautiful shade of a great elm-tree; and when you have looked upon its tall, majestic trunk, and its great and strong branches, with their ten thousand little limbs waving gracefully before the wind, you have been filled with admiration and delight. "What a mighty tree!" you say: "I wonder how long it has been growing." But the seed of that tree, when it was planted, many years ago, was no bigger than a mustard-seed; and if you had seen the little tiny sprout that your grandfather was tying up with so much care, when it was a few years old, you would have wondered that a man should think so much of such an insignificant twig. But, if he had let it grow up as it began, without any care, it never would have been the stately tree it is now. That was the most important period in its life, when it was a little twig. It began to lean over, and grow crooked and ugly. If it had not been trained up then, it would have continued to grow worse and worse; and, after it had grown to be a tree, it could not have been straightened at all. Now, you are, in some respects, like this little twig. You, too, have just begun to be; and now your character is pliable, like the young tree. But, unlike it, your being is to have no end. Instead of growing a few hundred years, like a great tree, you are to live for ever. And every thing that you do now must have an influence in forming your character for your whole being. In this latter sense, you cannot think too much of yourself; for you are the *germ* of an immortal being.

Did you ever stand by the shore of a placid lake or pond, in a calm, sunny day, and throw a little stone into its smooth, silvery waters? Did you observe how, first, a little ripple was formed around the place where it struck, and this was followed by a wave, and then, beyond, another, and another, till the whole surface of the water was disturbed? It was a very little thing that you did; and yet it agitated a great body of water. So it is with childhood and youth; the most insignificant action 'you perform, in its influence upon your character, will reach through the whole period of your existence.

It will not do for you to say, "It is no matter how I behave now; I shall do differently when I am a lady.' What you are while you are a girl, you will be when you become a woman. "But would you have a little girl act like a woman?" Not precisely. But I would have her act *like a lady*. Not to put on airs: not to put herself forward, and take the place of a woman before she is big enough to fill it: not to feel above labour, and despise those who perform it: not to look down with scorn upon every thing that is common: not to treat with contempt those who cannot dress as well as herself, or who have not seen so much of *style and fashion*. Those who behave so are *pseudo-ladies*. A *true lady* would despise such meanness. To *be a lady*, one must behave always with propriety; and be civil, courteous, and kind, to all. To treat any human being with rudeness, would show a want of breeding of which no *lady* would be guilty. But the romping, roisterous miss, who pays no regard to propriety of conduct, will never be a lady. You will not, however, misunderstand me. Do not suppose that I would have you dull and mopish, never manifesting any gayety of spirit or playfulness of conduct; but, in all these things, I would have you behave with strict regard to propriety.

Very young persons sometimes live in an *ideal world*,

What they imagine in their plays seems real. They have a little fairy world in their minds, in which they live more, and take greater delight, than they do in what is real and true. To this I do not object, within certain bounds; but often it becomes a *passion*, so that they lose all relish for sober every-day life. For such creatures of fancy, real life is too dull, and what concerns realities, too grave. Perhaps they will not like my book, because it treats of things true and real. But I beg them to consider that, through the whole of their being, they are to be concerned chiefly with *realities;* and therefore, to do them substantial good, we must speak to them of things real, and not of those airy things that belong to the fairy land. But real things are, truly, more interesting than the creations of fancy. The things of fancy interest you more, only because they appear new and less common. A person who has always lived in the country, and is used to sitting under the wide-spreading, shady tree, would be more pleased with the *picture* of a tree than with a *tree itself.* But one brought up in the city would cast away the picture, and hasten to enjoy the cool shade of the beautiful tree. A castle in the air may please the fancy; but you want a *real house* to live in.

CHAPTER II.

PERHAPS some of my readers, when they see the title of this chapter, will think only of confinement in school, of books, and of hard study, and so be inclined to pass over it, as a dry subject, which they have so much to do with, every day, that they have no wish to think of it in a moment of relaxation. But I beg them to stop a minute, and not throw me away, among the old school-books, till they have heard me through. I assure them that I use the term *education* in a far different sense. I think it means much more than going to school and studying books. This is only a small part of education. Mr. Walker defines education, "*The formation of manners in youth.*" But this is a very imperfect definition; and I am afraid there may be found some who would even doubt whether education has any thing to do with manners. Mr. Webster gives a better definition: "Education comprehends all that series of instruction and discipline which is intended to enlighten the understanding, correct the temper, and form the manners and habits of youth, and fit them for usefulness in their future stations;" all, in fact, that is necessary to make a MAN or a WOMAN, a GENTLEMAN or a LADY.

The original root, from which the word *education* is derived, means to *lead out*, to *conduct*, to *form*, to *fashion*, to *beat out*, to *forge*. It was used with reference to the forging of an instrument out of a piece of metal, or the chiselling of a statue out of a block of marble. This furnishes a good illustration of my ideas of *education*. It is a process by which a character is formed out of rude or unwrought materials. It is not confined to mere school learning. A person may be very *learned*, and yet not half *educated*. There are many steps in the process. The ore must first be dug up by the miner; then smelted at the furnace, and the metal separated from the dross; then wrought into bars at the foundry; afterwards forged by the smith; and then, finally, polished by the finisher. The marble must first be quarried, or blasted out of the ledge, then cut into blocks; then transported; then wrought with the hammer and chisel; and finally, polished. This gives a good idea of education. It is not merely what is done to form the character in *school;* but it comprises all the influences which are exerted upon the young, in training them up and forming their characters. Education begins in the *family*. It is carried forward in the *school*. It is affected, for good or for evil, by the influence of public worship, lectures, books, amusements, scenery, and companions. In all places and circumstances, something is doing towards the formation of character.

Yet there is one important respect in which *education*, or *the formation of character*, differs essentially from the process described in this illustration. The block of marble, or the piece of metal, is *passive;* the whole process is performed upon it by another. But no person can be educated in this way; every one that is educated must be *active*. You may be drilled through all the schools, and have every advantage at home and in society; and yet, without your own active co-operation, you can never be educated. But, if you are determined to be educated, you will turn every thing to some account. Every thing will be a school to you; for you will make contributions to your stock of knowledge from every object you see; and by seeking to act, discreetly, wisely, and correctly, in every place, you will be constantly forming good habits. Like the little busy bee, you will suck honey from every flower. You will commune with your own heart upon your bed, and exercise your powers of thought in useful meditation. You will converse with God in your secret place, and seek wisdom of Him who has promised to give liberally to those that ask. In company, you will be more ready to hear than to speak; and you will never meet with any so ignorant but you may learn from them some useful lessons. You will exercise your mind upon every person and object you meet. You will study philosophy in the fields, by the brooks, on the hills, in the valleys, and upon the broad canopy of heaven. It has been well observed, that the difference between a wise man and a fool is, that one goes through the world with his eyes wide open, while the other keeps them shut.

You will perceive, then, that your education is continually going on, whether you think of it or not. Your character is constantly forming. It is your business to keep out of the way of bad influences, and submit yourself to the moulding of the good. Keep in mind the great truth that you are forming a character for eternity. Some years ago, there were found on the banks of the Mississippi River the tracks of a human being, deeply imprinted in the solid rock. These tracks were made in the soft clay, which in time became hardened, and formed into stone; now the impression is immoveable. You now resemble this soft clay. Every thing with which you come in contact makes an impression. But, as you grow older, your character acquires solidity, and is less and less affected by these influences, till at length it will be like the hard stone, and the impressions made upon you at this season will become confirmed habits.

All the impressions made upon your character ought to be such as will not need to be removed. Washington Allston, the great painter, had been a long time at work on a most magnificent painting. He had nearly completed it, when his keen eye discovered some defects in a portion of the piece. He hastily drew his rough brush over that portion of the picture, intending to paint it anew. But in the midst of his plans, death seized him, and his painting remains, just as he left it. No other person can carry out the conception that was in his mind. If you allow wrong impressions to be made upon your forming character, death may meet you with his stern mandate, and fix them for ever, as immoveable as it left the rough print of the coarse brush upon Allston's canvass.

CHAPTER III.

A WATCH, to one who had never seen such a piece of mechanism before, would be a great wonder. It is an object of much curiosity to the natives of savage and barbarous tribes, visited by the missionaries. It seems to speak and move, as though instinct with life. I have read, somewhere, of a poor savage, who, seeing a white man's watch lying on the ground, and hearing it tick, supposed it to be some venomous reptile, and, with a stone, dashed it in pieces. A watch is an object of no less wonder to a child. Children are full of curiosity, as my readers well know. They wish to examine every thing they see; to take it in pieces, and see how it is made. I dare say my readers remember the time when they sat on their father's knee, and modestly requested him to show them the little wheels of his watch.

If I could sit down with my young friends, and take my watch in pieces, I would teach them a useful lesson. I would show them how a watch resembles a human being. There is the *case*, which may be taken off, and put by itself, and still the watch will go as well as ever. In this respect, it is like the human body. Death separates it from the soul, and yet the soul remains, with

3   B

all its active powers. It still lives. The inside of the watch, too, resembles the soul. It has a great many different parts, all working together in harmony; a great many wheels, all moving in concert. So the soul has a great many different powers or faculties, all designed to operate in concert with each other, as the *understanding*, the *judgment*, the *conscience*, the *will*, the *affections*, the *memory*, the *passions*, and the *desires;* and each one of these has a part to act, as important for the man as the several wheels and springs of the watch. If every part of the watch is in order, and in its proper place, it will keep exact time; but, if one wheel gets disordered, it will derange the whole. The secret power that moves the watch is unperceived. If you examine, you will see a large wheel, with a smooth surface, round which is wound a long chain, attached to another wheel, with ridges for the chain to run upon. Inside of the first-named wheel is the *main-spring*, which, by means of the chain, moves the whole machinery. The WILL is the main-spring of the soul. By a mysterious, invisible chain, it holds all the powers of the soul and body at its command. Not only the operations of the mind, but the motions of the body are controlled by the will.

But, if there were no check upon the main-spring of the watch, it would not give the time of day. It would set all the wheels in rapid motion, and in a few moments the watch would run down. To prevent this, there is a *balance-wheel*, which turns backwards and forwards, by means of a fine spring, called the *hair-spring*, and so keeps the whole machinery in a regular motion. To this is attached a little lever, called the *regulator*, which, by a gentle touch, works on this delicate spring, so as to move the balance-wheel faster or slower, as the case may be, to make the movement exact and regular.

Now, if there were no checks on the will, it would run on impetuously in its course, without regard to consequences. And this we often see in persons called *wilful, self-willed, headstrong.* Children are often so; if let alone, their stubborn will would lead them to rush on headlong to their own destruction. Without meaning to be very accurate in these illustrations, I shall call *judgment* the *balance-wheel.* This is the faculty which perceives, compares, and decides, keeps the mind balanced, and prevents its running to extremes either way.

The *hair-spring* and *regulator* of the watch I shall compare with *conscience.* A very slight touch of the regulator moves the hair-spring, and gives a quicker or a slower motion to the balance-wheel. But, if the watch is out of order, oftentimes the movement of the regulator has no effect upon it. So, when the soul is *in order,* a very slight touch of conscience will affect the judgment and regulate the will. But often, the soul is so much *out of order,* that conscience will have no effect upon it.

But who touches the regulator of the watch? There is nothing in the watch itself to do this. The power that moves the regulator *is applied to it.* So, the conscience is moved. The *Word of God* enlightens the conscience, and the *Spirit of God* applies the word. And this brings me to the point which I had in my mind when I began this chapter. What a poor thing a watch is, when it is out of order! It is of no use. A watch is made to keep the time of day; but, when it is out of order, it will keep no time. Or, if it is in order, and yet not regulated, it will not keep the right time.

Now until the heart is changed by the grace of God, the *soul is out of order.* It does not answer the purpose for which it was made. The *will* is wrong; the *judgment* is wrong; the *conscience* is wrong. And, whatever cultivation may be bestowed upon the mind, it will not act aright. In the very beginning, then, you want *piety*, as the *main-spring* of action, and the *regulator* of the soul. Without this, you are not prepared to begin any thing aright. Indeed, without it, you have no sufficient motive to action. You seem to be toiling and labouring and wearying yourself for nothing. But *piety towards God* gives a new impulse to the mind. When you set out to improve your mind, if you have no piety, the object to be gained by it is very small. It can secure to you no more than, perhaps, a little additional enjoyment, for the brief space you are to continue in this world. But piety opens to you a wide field of usefulness in this life, and the prospect of going forward in the improvement of your mind as long as eternity endures. It must, therefore, give a new spring and vigour to all the faculties of the soul. It does more. It *regulates* the powers of the mind, and the affections of the heart, and gives a right direction to them all.

I would persuade you, then, as the first and great thing, to *seek God*. Remember what Christ has said: " Seek ye first the kingdom of God and his righteousness, and all these things shall be added unto you." Here is the promise that you shall have all else that is needful, if you seek God first. Yield your heart to him, and have his kingdom set up there. Let him rule in your heart, and devote yourself to his service, and he will supply all your need. This, also, will give a right direction to all your faculties, and lay a good foundation of character. But, without it, you will be like a watch without a balance-wheel or a regulator; you will be fit neither for this life nor that which is to come. And, it is of the utmost importance that you should become pious now, while you are young. If you would form a good character, you must have a good foundation laid at the beginning. Nothing but this can make a good foundation. All your habits ought to be formed and settled upon religious principles. Religious motives should enter into all your efforts to improve your mind and cultivate your affections. And, should you neglect religion now, and afterwards, by the grace of God, be led to devote yourself to him, you will find it hard and difficult to overcome the wrong habits of mind and conduct which you will have formed.

Piety, then, is the first thing to be considered, in the *formation of character*. And remember, also, that you are forming character *for eternity;* and that your whole being, through a never ending existence, is to be affected by the character which you form now in your childhood and youth. If you lay the foundation of your character now in the love and fear of God, it will rise higher and higher, in excellence, beauty, and loveliness, for ever and ever. But if you lay the foundation in selfishness and sin, and build accordingly, it will for ever be sinking lower in degradation and deeper in wretchedness.

Illustrations.

LET no light-hearted girl pass this over because it begins with a grave subject. There is nothing in it which interferes with any proper youthful enjoyment. I am sorry that any one should think religion tends to destroy the happiness of children and youth. This is not true. It does, indeed, forbid all sinful indulgence; but at the same time it removes the desire for it; and it introduces them to pleasures of a more exalted kind. Let no one say, "I will have my pleasure now, and attend to religion when I am a woman." Perhaps you will not live to be a woman. But, if you should, you want religion now, to lay the foundation of a good character. When the prophet Elisha was living at Jericho, some of the people came to him, and told him that the water was very bad. Now, the city of Jericho was supplied with water from a spring, which was conducted to the city, I suppose, in an aqueduct of some kind. And what did the prophet do? He did not go to the streams, which conveyed the water to different parts of the city, to see if he could purify them; but he went and cast salt into the spring, and the water was made good. This is what you must do: cast salt into the spring, that the stream of life may run pure. You want your heart purified by the influence of true piety, in order that your character may be formed upon the true model.

Neither let any one think, that there is greater difficulty in becoming a Christian in childhood, than there is at a later period of life. There is much less. If any one wanted a tree in front of his house, would he go and dig up and transplant a great tree, with a tall, heavy trunk, wide-spreading branches, and great roots running deep into the ground? He might possibly do it; but it would be a work of great difficulty, and the tree would not be very likely to live. He would rather choose a young tree, which would be easily and safely transplanted. In like manner, the difficulty of becoming religious increases as one grows older.

A woman of ninety lay on her death-bed, who had been a disciple of Christ for half a century. Conversing with a friend, she said, "Tell all the children that an old woman, who is just on the borders of eternity, is very much grieved that she did not begin to love the Saviour when she was a child. Tell them that youth is the time to serve the Lord."

Neither let any one get the impression, that all pious children die when they are young. Most of the children's memoirs that have been written are necessarily accounts of those who died young. But thousands of children have died whose memoirs have not been written; and a great many die without giving any evidence of piety, which is a much greater cause of alarm to you, than that some pious children die. But children are no more likely to die because they are pious. Many, who have become pious in childhood, have lived to a very great age. Phebe Bartlett, of whose early piety a most delightful account was given by President Edwards, lived to be seventy-four years of age. Indeed, the tendency of true piety is to promote health and long life.

A LITTLE GIRL'S RELIGIOUS EXPERIENCE.

THE following sweet and simple expression of early piety was presented to the Church in Stratham, New Hampshire, nearly forty years ago, by a little girl about eleven years of age, who lived many years to adorn the profession which she then made, by an exemplary piety and Christian conversation.

"My dear and honoured parents had often told me, when I was preparing to go to meeting, that I ought to attend to the religious exercises, and at least to remember the text. On the Lord's day last summer, as I was going to meeting, I recollected my mother's advice, and had a great desire, and some strong resolutions, to attend, and at least to carry the text home with me; but I think I shall never forget it. These solemn words, 'How shall we escape, if we neglect so great salvation?' seem to be imprinted on my heart, and will not, I trust, be soon blotted out of my memory. I think I felt the truth of every word that was said in the sermon. I am sure I saw that the salvation of Jesus is a great salvation, and that it was very wicked to neglect it, and as dangerous as it was wicked. And I was very sensible, that, though I was a young sinner, I needed that great salvation, as really as the oldest sinner in the meeting-house. I was very sure I had wickedly neglected it. Returning home, I could not help thinking of the text and sermon. Nor could I help reproaching myself for my wicked neglect of Jesus and his great salvation.

"After this, I attended lectures whenever I could, and thought all the awful and solemn warnings of the word of God were directed to me, as really as if I had been named. I heard those alarming words, 'Depart, ye cursed, into everlasting fire, prepared for the devil and his angels.' And this awful sentence I believed would be directed against all who lived in sin, and died destitute of love to God and the Lord Jesus Christ. I found I had no love to God, no love to Jesus; and was certain, that if I lived and died so, God would say to me, 'Depart.' The thought distressed me. I could not bear to think of being banished from God. I wanted to know and love God. I asked for mercy. My heart, I saw, was wicked, and must be changed, or God could not love me. I found I could not change it myself, and I tried to pray that God would renew my hard and sinful heart. I saw, too, that I could not merit his favour, that my prayers could not help me, nor oblige the Lord to save me. I found myself altogether helpless, and lying at the mercy of God. And, for ever blessed be his name, he led me to trust in his mercy, in the Lord Jesus Christ. I had, I think, some clear views of Jesus, as the Saviour, who alone can save a sinner so unworthy as I saw myself to be. I think I enjoy a measure of the peace and comfort which flow from a reliance on his glorious grace alone. And, though I have had many doubts and fears, I have also many sweet and refreshing seasons.

"And now, Jesus Christ is so precious to my soul, his religion is so refreshing to my mind, and his ordinances are so lovely in my view, that I wish and long to enjoy access to them. I cannot but anxiously desire to give myself up to God, and to his Church, in the bonds of his own everlasting covenant. And now, while I ask your love, I also beg your prayers to God, that he would own me as a child of his, in that day when he will make up his jewels."

You will perceive, from this narrative, that religion is not gloomy and repulsive. It fits the mind for true enjoyment. It gives a person the only true ground of cheerfulness, which is, a mind at peace with God. When embraced in childhood, it lays the foundation of character upon a solid basis. It gives it stability, by fixing in the heart true principles of action, and giving a love for what is right, and a dislike for what is wrong.

CHAPTER IV.

NEXT to your duty to God comes your duty to your *parents;* and you can never form an excellent, amiable, and lovely character, unless the foundation of it is laid in *filial piety,* as well as in piety towards God. Solomon says to the young, "Hear the instruction of thy father, and forsake not the law of thy mother; for they shall be an ornament of grace unto thy head, and chains about thy neck." Nothing will make you appear so lovely in the eyes of others as a dutiful behaviour towards your parents; and nothing will make you appear so unamiable and unlovely as a disrespectful, disobedient carriage towards them. No ornament sits so gracefully upon youth as filial piety; no outward adorning can compare with it.

Filial piety calls into exercise feelings towards your parents, similar to those which piety towards God calls into exercise towards him; such as esteem and veneration of his character, love to his person, confidence in his word, submission to his authority, and penitence for offences against him. When the heart is habituated to the exercise of these feelings towards parents, it is prepared the more readily to exercise them towards God. The promises which God has made to those who honour their parents, and his threatenings against those who dishonour them, are similar to those which he has made respecting honour and obedience to himself. You owe it, therefore, to God, to exercise filial piety, because he has required it, and because it is one of the means he employs to cultivate piety towards himself. *Gratitude*, also, should lead to filial piety, as well as to piety towards God; for what God is to man, only in a lower sense, the parent is to his child. Your parents are, under God, the authors of your being. The greater part of parents' lives is spent in rearing, supporting, and educating their children. For this they wear out their strength in anxious care and toil; they watch beside the bed of their children when they are sick, with tender solicitude and sleepless vigilance; they labour to provide for them. But good parents are, most of all, anxious that their children should grow up intelligent and virtuous, pious and happy. There is no being but God to whom children are so much indebted as to a faithful parent; and almost all the blessings that God bestows upon them come through their parents.

Filial piety has great influence on future character. One who has never been in the habit of submitting to others, will always be headstrong and self-willed; and such a character no body loves. You cannot always do as you please; and, if such is your disposition, you will always be unhappy when your will is crossed. You will be unwilling to submit to necessary restraints, and this will irritate, and keep you in misery; for you will never see the time in your life when you will be so entirely independent of others that you can have your own way in every thing. Even the king on his throne cannot do this. But, if you have always been in the habit of submitting to your parents, these necessary restraints will be no burden. If, then, you would be respected, beloved, and happy, when you grow up and take your place in society, you must *honour your parents.* Cultivate the habit of submission to their authority; of respectful attention to their instructions; and of affection and reverence to their persons. These are the habits that will make you respected, beloved, and happy. But as God has joined a curse to parental impiety, so he makes it punish itself. And thus you will find that it is generally followed with the most dreadful consequences. Of this I might give many painful examples; but the narratives would swell my book to an immoderate size.

The whole duty of children to parents, is expressed by God himself in one word: HONOUR. This word is chosen, with great felicity, to express all the various duties of children toward their parents. There is a great deal of meaning in this little word, *honour.*

Do you ask, *" How shall I honour my parents?"* In the first place, you must honour them *in your heart,* by loving and reverencing them, and by cultivating a submissive, obedient disposition. It is not honouring your parents to indulge an unsubmissive, turbulent spirit. To be angry with your parents, and to feel that their lawful commands are hard or unreasonable, is dishonouring them. The authority which God has given your parents over you is for your good, that they may restrain you from evil and hurtful practices, and require you to do what will be, in the end, for your benefit. When they restrain you, or require you to do what is not pleasing to you, they have a regard to your best interests. To be impatient of restraint, and to indulge hard feelings toward them, is doing them great dishonour. If you could read the hearts of your parents, and see what a struggle it costs them to interfere with your inclinations, you would feel differently.

But these rebellious feelings of yours are not only against your parents, but against God, who gave them this authority over you.

Children also honour or dishonour their parents by their *words*. You honour them, by addressing them in respectful language, and in a tone of voice indicating reverence and submission, giving them those titles that belong to their superior station. An example of this we have in the answer of Samuel to what he supposed the call of Eli: "Here am I:" a form of speech used by servants to their masters, and implying attention to what was said, and a readiness to execute what was commanded. But parents are dishonoured, when their children answer them gruffly, or speak in a sharp, positive, angry, or self-important tone; or when they neglect to accompany their address with the usual titles of respect, but speak out bluntly, "*Yes,*" or "*No.*" This shows the state of the heart. And I think the reason why it is so difficult, in these days, to teach children to say, "Yes, sir," and "No, ma'am," is, that they do not feel in their hearts the respect which these terms imply. You will perceive, by this remark, that I have no respect for the notion which prevails, in some quarters, that these expressions are not genteel.

Children likewise dishonour their parents, when they answer back, and argue against their commands, or excuse themselves for not obeying. It is as much as to say, they are wiser than their parents: which is doing them a great dishonour. To speak to them in disrespectful, reproachful, or passionate language, or to speak of them or their authority in such language to others, is also a great offence against their honour. Under the law of Moses, God punished this offence in the same manner that he punished blasphemy against himself:

"He that curseth his father or his mother shall surely be put to death." This shows what a great offence it is in his sight.

Another way in which you honour your parents is, by giving respectful attention to their instruction and counsels. God has committed your instruction and training to them; and when they teach or advise you according to the Scripture, their instructions are the voice of God to you. If you despise their instruction, you cast contempt upon God, who speaks through them, and who says, "My son, hear the instruction of thy father, and forsake not the law of thy mother." It is very natural for children to wish to follow their own inclinations. The impetuosity of youth would hurry them on, heedlessly, in the high-road to ruin. And, often, they despise the wholesome instruction and advice of their parents, as only designed to interfere with their pleasures, and abridge their enjoyments; while, in truth, their parents look beyond *mere pleasure*, to that which is of greater importance. They look upon these things in the light which age and experience has given them. If you were going to a strange place, in a way with which you were not acquainted, and should meet one that had been that way before, you would put confidence in what he should tell you of the way, and follow his directions. Your parents have passed through the period of life on which you are now entering, and they know the way. You will do well to confide in them, and abide by their instructions. If you neglect to do so, you will be sure to get into difficulty. The path of life is beset, on every side, with by-paths, leading astray; and these by-paths are full of snares and pit-falls, to catch the unwary, and plunge them into ruin. Your parents have become acquainted with these ways, and know their dangers. If they are good people, and understand their duty to you, they will warn you against them; and it will be the height of folly for you to disregard their warnings. Multitudes, by doing so, have rushed heedlessly on to ruin.

You must honour your parents, also, by a *prompt and cheerful obedience* to their lawful commands. I say *lawful*, because no one ought to obey a command to do what is positively wrong. If a wicked parent should command his child to break the Sabbath, to lie, or to steal, or to break any of God's commands, it would be the child's duty to refuse, and meekly submit to the punishment which the parent might inflict. It is not often that such things happen among us; but our missionaries in Constantinople have related two instances that are in point. Two little Armenian girls had learned to read, and obtained from the missionaries some ideas of Christian morality. A person knocked at the door of their house, and their father, not wishing to see him, told one of them to go and tell the person that he was *not at home.* "That would be telling a lie," said the daughter. "What then?" said the father; "it is a very little thing. You have only to say that I am not at home." "But, father," she replied, "the Bible says it is wicked to tell lies, and I cannot tell a lie." He was angry, and called his other daughter, and told her to go. She replied, "Father, I cannot, for it is wicked to lie." These children did right in refusing to obey such a command. But in no other case, except when told to do what is wrong, will a child be justified in refusing to obey.

Obedience must be *prompt* and *cheerful.* Your parents are not honoured, when obedience is delayed to suit your convenience; nor when you *answer back,* or try to *reason against* your parents' commands, or plead for delay, that you may first finish your own work. A parent who is honoured will never have to repeat the same command. Some children are bent on having their own way, and attempt to carry their point by showing their parents that their way is best; which is the same as saying to them that they are more ignorant than their children. Neither is *sullen obedience* honouring your parents. Some children, who dare not disobey their parents, will go about doing what is required of them with great reluctance, with perhaps a sullen expression of the countenance, a flirt, an angry step, or a slam of the door, or some other show of passion. Such conduct is a grief to parents, and an offence against God, who will not count that as obedience, which is not done cheerfully. But if you truly honour your parents from the heart, you will not wait for their *commands.* You will be always ready to obey the slightest intimation of their wishes. It is a great grief to a parent, when, out of respect to his child's feelings, he has expressed his *wish,* to be obliged to add his *command,* before the thing will be done. But filial piety never appears so amiable and lovely as when it anticipates the wishes of parents, and supersedes the necessity of expressing those wishes in advice or commands.

If you honour your parents in your heart, you will pay an equal regard to their counsels and commands, whether they are present or absent. If you cast off their authority as soon as you are out of their sight, you greatly dishonour them. Such conduct shows that you do not honour them at all in your heart, but obey them only when you cannot disobey without suffering for it. But if you keep their authority always present with you, then you will do them great honour; for you show that they have succeeded in fixing in your heart a deep-seated principle of reverence and affection for them.   If you truly honour your parents *in your heart,* you will obey them as well when they are absent as present.   The parents' authority and honour are always present with the good child.

Children, likewise, honour or dishonour their parents in their *general behaviour.* If they are rude and uncivil, they reflect dishonour upon their parents; for people say, they have not been trained and instructed at home. But when their behaviour is respectful, correct, pure, and amiable, it reflects honour upon the parents. People will judge of the character of your parents by your behaviour.   Are you willing to hear your parents reproachfully spoken of?   No, your cheek would glow with indignation at the person who should speak ill of your father or your mother.   But you speak evil of them, in your conduct, every time you do any thing that reflects dishonour upon them in the eyes of others. The blame of your conduct will be thrown back upon your parents.

But the true way to honour your parents, at all times and in all circumstances, is, to have your heart right with God.   If you have true piety of heart toward God, you will show piety toward your parents; for you will regard the authority of his commandment, and delight in doing what will please him.   The fear of God, dwelling in your heart, will lead you to reverence all his commands, and none more continually and conscientiously than the one which requires you to honour your parents.   Every thing that you do for them will be done, " not with eye-service, as men-pleasers, but with good will, doing service as to God, and not to man."

Filial piety adds a peculiar charm to the female character; while the want of it, in females, makes them appear like monsters.   Disobedience, or the want of proper respect and reverence to parents, is so contrary to the gentle nature of your sex, that it makes them appear very unlovely. This defect needs but to be seen in a girl or a young lady, to spoil all her attractions. No matter how beautiful she is, this defect will be a *black spot* on her pretty face; no matter how much she *knows*, her knowledge, if it does not lead her to honour her parents, only "puffeth up;" no matter how genteel she may be in her behaviour to others, the first step in gentility is, respectful and obedient carriage towards parents. True gentility comes from gentleness of heart; but there can be no gentleness in that female's heart who dishonours her parents. No matter with how much elegance and taste she may decorate her beautiful form, this defect will make her appear worse than the most deformed person, clad in tattered garments made up of dirty old shreds and patches. Nor will it be confined to childhood and youth; there is, perhaps, nothing that has a more important bearing upon the future character of children and youth than their treatment of their parents. God has set a mark upon it; a good one, upon filial piety, but the mark of Cain upon filial impiety. This latter will stick to you, like a deep, broad scar upon your pretty face, or a permanent deformity in your naturally fine form. But a quick perception of propriety, in regard to the respect due to parents, with a constant watchfulness to show attention, and to anticipate their wants, will adorn a young lady, in the view of all beholders, more than all the finery, and jewels, and other ornaments, that can be heaped upon her. It will make her appear more beautiful than the finest form that was ever beheld, or the most comely countenance that was ever reflected in a mirror.

Illustrations.

FILIAL PIETY.

MY readers will perceive why I have chosen this for my next subject; because piety towards parents is the next thing to piety towards God. Indeed, it is one of its first fruits. And I can hardly think it possible that a child can be pious towards God, and irreverent and disobedient towards her parents; for parents stand, in an important sense, to children, in the place of God. He has committed you to their care, to bring up for him. The following examples furnish some forcible illustrations of the subject of filial piety.

THE FAITHFUL DAUGHTER.

DURING the French Revolution, M. Delleglaie, who had been confined in prison at Lyons, was ordered to Paris. His daughter begged to be allowed to ride with him, but was refused. Though of very delicate health, she followed him on foot, a distance of more than three hundred miles, preparing him food, and providing covering for him, in the dungeons where he was confined at night. At Paris, for three months, she presented herself before the authorities, in his behalf, till, at length, she prevailed, and procured his release. She conducted him back to Lyons. But the effort was too much for her; and having gained her object, and saved the life of her father, she lost her own.

FILIAL PIETY REWARDED.

A FEMALE servant in London, in her early life, spent all her wages in the support of her aged and distressed parents. She was afterwards taken ill; and the Rev. Thomas Scott, to whose congregation she belonged, with the aid of kind friends, supported her for many years, by which she was saved from going to the workhouse. Thus was she rewarded for her dutiful conduct towards her parents.

LADY LUCY'S PETITION.

THE following touching narrative of a historical fact contains such a beautiful illustration of filial piety as to need no comment. When I commenced this book, one of my children, on learning my intention, inquired, "Father, are you going to *make comments* on your anecdotes, or *leave them to tell their own story?*" In regard to this one, I shall *leave it to tell its own story.*

James II. King of England, was a great tyrant. He disregarded the constitution and laws of England, and undertook to exercise arbitrary and absolute power. Among other tyrannical and oppressive

measures, he undertook to restore Popery as the estab.
lished religion. The People of England could not bear
these things; and they entered into a negotiation with
William, Prince of Orange, who had married the king's
daughter Mary, to come over from Holland with an
army, when they all joined him, and King James was
obliged to leave the country; after which, the Parlia-
ment raised William and Mary to the throne. James
and his friends made several ineffectual attempts to
recover his crown. In one of these attempts, Lord
Preston was engaged; and, being taken, was condemned
to die. His little daughter, Lucy, was taken by her
nurse, Amy Gradwell, to visit her father, in the Tower,
before his execution. As the coach drove up before
the prison, Lady Lucy raised her eyes fearfully to the
Tower, and exclaimed, "And is my dear papa shut up
in this dismal place, to which you are taking me,
nurse?" When they alighted, and she saw the soldiers
on guard, and the sentinels before the prison, she
trembled and hid her face in Amy's cloak. "Yes, my
dear child," replied her nurse, "my lord, your father,
is indeed within these sad walls. You are now going
to visit him. Are you afraid to enter this place, my
dear?" "No," replied Lady Lucy, resolutely, "I am
not afraid of going to any place where my dear papa
is." Yet she clung closer to the arm of her attendant,
as she entered the gloomy precincts of the building, and
her little heart fluttered fearfully, as she glanced around
her; and she whispered to her nurse, "Was it not here
that the two young princes, Edward V., and his brother
Richard, Duke of York, were murdered by their cruel
uncle, Richard, Duke of Gloucester?"

"Yes, my love, it was; but do not be alarmed on
that account, for no one will harm you," said Amy, in
an encouraging tone. "And was not good Henry VI.

murdered, also, by the same wicked Richard?" continued the little girl, whose imagination had been filled with the deeds of blood that had been perpetrated in this fatally celebrated place; many of which had been related to her by Bridget, the housekeeper, since her father had been imprisoned in the Tower on the charge of high treason.

"But do you think they will murder papa, nurse?" "Hush! hush! dear child, you must not talk these things here," said Amy, "or they will shut us both up in a room with bolts and bars, instead of admitting us to see my lord, your father."

Lady Lucy pressed closer to her nurse's side, and was silent, till they were ushered into the room where her father was confined; when, forgetting every thing else in the joy of seeing him again, she sprang into his arms, and almost stifled him with her kisses. Lord Preston was greatly affected at the sight of his little daughter; and, overcome by her passionate expressions of fondness, his own anguish at the thought of being separated from her by death, and the idea of leaving her an orphan at the tender age of nine years, he clasped her to his bosom, and bedewed her face with his tears. "Why do you cry, dear papa?" asked Lucy, who was herself weeping at the sight of his distress. "And why do you not leave this gloomy place, and come home to your own hall again?"

"Attend to me, Lucy," said her father, "and I will tell you the cause of my grief: I shall never come home again, for I have been condemned to die for high treason; and I shall not leave this place, till they bring me forth to Tower Hill, where they will cut off my head with a sharp axe, and set it up afterwards over Temple Bar or London Bridge."

At this terrible intelligence, Lucy screamed aloud,

and hid her face in her father's bosom, which she wet with her tears. "Be composed, my dear child," said her father, "for I have much to say to you; and we may never meet again in this world." "No, no, dear papa! they shall not kill you; for I will cling so fast about your neck, that they cannot cut your head off; and I will tell them all how good and kind you are; and then they will not want to kill you." "My dearest love, all this would be of no use," said her father. "I have offended against the law, by trying to have my old master, King James, restored to the throne. Lucy, do you not remember that I once took you to Whitehall, to see King James, and how kindly he spoke to you?"

O, yes, papa! and I recollect he laid his hand on my head, and said I was like what his daughter, the Princess of Orange, was at my age;" replied Lucy, with great animation.

"Well, my child, very soon after you saw King James at Whitehall, the Prince of Orange, who had married his daughter, came over to England, and drove King James out of his palace and kingdom; and the people made him and the Princess of Orange king and queen in his stead."

"But was it not very wicked of the Princess to take her father's kingdom away from him? I am very sorry King James thought me like her," said Lucy earnestly.

"Hush, hush, my love! You must not speak so of the Queen. Perhaps she thought she was doing right to deprive her father of his kingdom, because he had embraced the Catholic religion; and it is against the law for a king of England to be a Catholic. Yet, I confess, I did not think she would consent to sign the death-warrant of so many of her father's old servants, only on account of their faithful attachment to him," said he, with a sigh.

"I have heard that the Princess of Orange is of a merciful disposition," said old Amy Gradwell, "and perhaps she might be induced to spare your life, my lord, if your pardon were very earnestly entreated of her, by some of your friends."

"Alas! my good Amy, no one will undertake the perilous office of pleading for a traitor, lest he should be suspected of favouring King James."

"Dear papa, let me go to the Queen, and beg your pardon," cried Lucy, with a crimsoned cheek and sparkling eye. "I will so beg and pray her to spare your life, dear father, that she will not have the heart to deny me."

"Dear simple child! What could you say to the Queen that would be of any avail?"

"God would teach me what to say," replied Lucy. Her father clasped her to his bosom. "But," said he, "thou wouldst be afraid of speaking to the Queen, even should you be admitted to her presence, my child."

"Why should I be afraid of speaking to her, papa? Should she be angry with me, and answer me harshly, I shall be thinking too much of you to care about it; and if she should send me to the Tower, and cut off my head, God will take care of my immortal soul."

"You are right, my child, to fear God, and have no other fear. He, perhaps, has put it into thy little heart to plead for thy father's life; which if it be his pleasure to grant, I shall indeed feel it a happiness, that my child should be the instrument of my deliverance. If it should be otherwise, God's will be done. He will not forsake my good and dutiful little one, when I am laid low in the dust."

"But how will my lady Lucy gain admittance to the

Queen's presence ?" asked old Amy, who had been a weeping spectator of this interesting scene.

"I will write a letter to my friend, the Lady Clarendon, requesting her to accomplish the matter," said Lord Preston. He then wrote a few hasty lines, which he gave to his daughter, telling her that she was to go to the palace the next day, properly attended, and give the letter to Lady Clarendon, who was there waiting upon the Queen. He then kissed his child tenderly, and bade her farewell. Though Lucy wept as she parted from her father, yet she left the Tower with a far more quiet mind than she had entered it; for she had formed her resolution, and her young heart was full of hope. The next morning, the little Lady Lucy was up before the lark, dressed in a suit of deep mourning; and as she passed through the hall, leaning on her nurse's arm, and attended by her father's confidential secretary and the old butler, all the servants shed tears, and prayed that God would bless and prosper her. Lady Lucy was introduced to Lady Clarendon's apartments before she had left her bed; and having told her artless story with great earnestness, presented her father's letter.

Lady Clarendon was very kind to little Lucy, but told her plainly that she did not dare to ask her father's life, because her husband was already suspected of holding secret correspondence with his brother-in-law, King James. "O," said Lucy, "if I could only see the Queen myself, I would not wish any one to speak for me. I would plead so earnestly, that she could not refuse me, I am sure."

"Poor child! What could you say to the Queen?"

"God will direct me what to say," replied Lucy.

"Well, my love, you shall have the opportunity;

but much I fear your little heart will fail, when you see the Queen face to face."

The Countess hastened to rise and dress, and then conducted Lucy into the palace gallery, where the Queen usually passed an hour in walking, early in the morning. While they were waiting for the Queen, Lady Clarendon tried to amuse little Lucy, by showing her the pictures which hung on the wall. "I know that gentleman well," said Lucy, pointing to a full-length portrait of James II. "That is a portrait of Queen Mary's father," said the Countess. "But hark! here comes the Queen with her ladies. Now, Lucy, is the time. I will step into the recess, yonder; but you must remain alone, standing where you are. When the Queen approaches, kneel and present your father's petition. She who walks before the other ladies is the Queen. Be of good courage."

Lady Clarendon then made a hasty retreat. Lucy's heart beat violently, when she found herself alone; but her resolution did not fail her. She stood with folded hands, pale but composed, and motionless as a statue, awaiting the Queen's approach; and when the Queen came near, she advanced a step forward, dropped on her knees, and presented the petition.

The extreme beauty of the child, her deep mourning, the touching sadness of her look and manner, and, above all, the streaming tears that bedewed her cheek, excited the Queen's attention and interest. She paused, spoke kindly to her, and took the offered paper; but when she saw the name of Lord Preston, her colour rose, she frowned, cast the petition from her, and would have passed on; but Lucy, who had watched her countenance with an anxiety which almost amounted to agony, losing all awe for royalty in her fears for her father, put forth her hand, and, grasping the Queen's robe, cried in an imploring tone, "Spare my father! my dear, dear father, royal lady!"

Lucy had meant to say many persuasive things; but in her sore distress she forgot them all, and could only repeat, "Save my father, gracious Queen!" till her feelings choked her voice, and throwing her arms round the Queen's knees, she leaned her head against her person, and sobbed aloud. Queen Mary pitied the distress of her young petitioner; but she considered the death of Lord Preston a measure of political necessity, because he was a ringleader in a conspiracy to overturn the government, and bring back King James, her father, to the throne. She therefore told Lucy mildly, but firmly, that she could not grant her request.

"But he is good and kind to every one," said Lucy, raising her blue eyes, which were swimming in tears, to the face of the Queen. "He may be so to you, child," returned the Queen; "but he has broken the laws of his country, and therefore he must die."

"But you *can* pardon him," replied Lucy, "and I have learned that God has said, 'Blessed are the merciful, for they shall obtain mercy.'"

"It does not become a little child like you to attempt to instruct me," replied the Queen gravely; "I am acquainted with my duty. It is my place to administer justice impartially, and it is not possible for me to pardon your father, however painful it may be to deny so dutiful a child."

Lucy did not reply; she only raised her eyes with an appealing look to the Queen, and then turned them expressly on the portrait of King James. This excited the Queen's curiosity, and she inquired of Lucy why she gazed so intently upon that picture. "I was thinking," replied Lucy, "how very strange it is, that you should wish to kill *my* father, only because he loved *yours* so faithfully."

This wise and artless reproof from so young a child, went to the very heart of the Queen. She raised her eyes to that once dear and honoured parent who had ever been a tender father to her; and when she thought of him as an exile in a foreign land, relying upon the bounty of strangers for his daily bread, while she was invested with the royalty of which he had been deprived, the contrast between herself and the pious and dutiful child before her affected her heart, and she burst into tears. "Rise, dear child," said she, "I cannot make thee an orphan. Thou hast prevailed. Thy father shall not die. Thy filial love has saved him!"

CHAPTER V.

THE happiness of a family depends very much on the conduct of the daughters. They can make home sweet and pleasant. If they are sweet tempered and amiable, kind and obliging, they will always make it sunshine about them. But if they are peevish and fretful, selfish and quarrelsome, they will make home as cold and cheerless as a north-east storm. To make home a pleasant sunshiny place, the family must be governed by the golden rule. If the daughters govern themselves by it, they will be able to shed about the fire-side an air of cheerfulness and benignity that will charm every one who comes within the circle of its influence.

If you are the eldest sister, your situation in the family is one of considerable importance and responsibility. Your conduct and example will have a great influence upon your younger brothers and sisters. But you must guard against making too much of this distinction, and expecting too much deference to be paid to you on account of it. You will be tempted to be overbearing and tyrannical in your demeanour toward them. You must guard against this. Your situation in the family, though it entitles you to some deference and respect, yet does not give you any authority; and therefore you must maintain it by the arts of persuasion and kindness. All attempts to domineer over your younger brothers and sisters, will only lead them to treat your pretensions with contempt. But if you speak kindly to them, and show yourself ready to oblige them, and help them out of their little difficulties, you will acquire an influence over them that will be better than authority. It is said that an elephant may be *led* by a single hair; but I need not tell you how vain must be any attempt to *drive* him. Be always good natured, gentle, and kind. Never speak in a cross tone, nor with an assuming air, and never *command* them. By such means you will secure their *affections*, which will bind them to you with a silken cord. And if you never lead them astray, you will also secure their *confidence* to strengthen this cord. Then you may lead them by it at your pleasure.

If you are a younger sister, you must pay some deference to your brothers and sisters older than yourself. If you have an older brother, always treat him respectfully and confidingly. Endeavour to secure his affections and confidence, so that he will be your guide and protector whenever you need. Be kind and gentle toward him, always yielding to his wishes, whenever you can do so with propriety, never setting up your own will against his, for the sake of having your own way; and be not particular about your own rights. Never behave pettishly toward him, nor find needless faults with him. A sister's power over her brothers lies in her gentleness and sweetness of temper. If you always show an amiable, sweet, loving disposition, they will love you, and seek to gratify your wishes. But if you attempt to carry your point by contention, they will shun you, as one who only interferes with their enjoyment.

Make a friend and confidant of your eldest sister. Consult her wishes, and yield to her, when any difference arises between you.

And, in general, sisters should be angels of mercy and peace in a family; gentle, kind, affectionate, tender, and good natured, toward all. Make it an invariable rule never to contend; and if you see the beginning of strife, always be the peace-maker; act the part of a mediator, by offering your services to bring about a good understanding between those that are at variance. Never raise your voice so high as to give it the appearance of harshness. Suppress the first risings of angry feeling, remembering that "anger resteth in the bosom of fools." Never speak unkindly to your brothers or sisters; and if they speak unkindly to you, do not suffer yourself to be irritated, and to answer back in an angry tone, but show your superiority by controlling your feelings. Be helpful to all about you. If your little brother comes in cold, or wet, or tired, assist him to a seat, take off his outer garments, warm his hands, and make him comfortable. If your little sister is grieved or in trouble, do not speak harshly to her, or reproach her for crying, but try to soothe her feelings by diverting her attention. Never teaze your brothers or sisters: you do not like to be teazed; then do not teaze others. Be courteous: do not speak coarsely or roughly, as ill-bred children do to each other, but be a lady, and treat your brothers and sisters like little gentlemen and ladies. Employ no coarse jokes or vulgar jests. Be careful of their feelings. Never do any thing needlessly, to interfere with their plans, to cross their feelings, or to hold them up to the ridicule of others; and play no tricks upon them. Such things will diminish their affection, and they will seize the first opportunity to retaliate. Be not fond of informing against them. If they commit any great offence against your parents' authority, it will be your duty to inform them of it. But then you should do it in a very careful manner, not exaggerating, or making it worse than it is, nor speaking of it exultingly or harshly; but show by your manner that you are really sorry for the necessity you are under of performing a painful duty. But, in matters of little consequence, it is better for you to remonstrate kindly and tenderly with them, but not to appeal to your parents. If you do, it will occur so frequently that you will get the settled ill-will of your brothers and sisters. In some families you can hear little else, when all the children are at home, but "Mother, James!" "Mother, Mary!" "Mother, Thomas!" "Mother, Sarah!" a perpetual string of complaints, that makes the place more like a bedlam than a quiet sweet home. If your little brother comes along in a pettish mood, and gives you a gentle slap, half in earnest and half in fun, do not cry out, *"Mother, John's pounding me!"* but take no notice of it, and presently, when he gets better natured, he will be sorry, and perhaps come of his own accord and ask your pardon; or at least, show by infallible signs that he wants to *make friends* with you. But if you bristle up, and make a great ado about it, you will have trouble enough. There is no sight more unlovely than a quarrelsome family, no place on earth more undesirable than a family of brothers and sisters, who are perpetually contending with one another. But there is no place this side heaven so sweet and attractive as a family of brothers and sisters always smiling and happy, full of kindness and love, delighting in each other's happiness, and striving how much each can oblige the other.

3

D

But perhaps you are an *only child*. Then you will
not have some of the trials common to youth. You
will not have to strive against those clashing interests
and feelings which exist in a large family of brothers
and sisters. Your temper will not be put to such
trials. But these trials are necessary, in order to discipline the heart, and to teach you the duties growing out
of the different relations in life; and you will have
them first to encounter abroad, when you come in
contact with other girls. You will be greatly in danger
of becoming selfish and consequential. Having no
rival in your parents' affections and attentions, you will
naturally feel as if you were a person of some consequence, and will, very likely, set a higher value upon
yourself than your companions will be willing to
acknowledge. Nothing is more liable to give young
persons false notions of their own superiority than
being brought up alone, with no opportunity to contrast themselves daily with others near their own age.

Be generous in your treatment of domestics. Nothing appears more unlovely than to see a pert little
miss domineering over a woman who is employed in
doing the work of the house. It is mean and despicable. Such persons have many unpleasant duties to
perform; and it should be your aim to render their
situation as agreeable and pleasant as possible. Never
presume to *command* them. This does not belong to
you. If you need their help, request it as a favour;
but never ask them to do any thing for you which you
can do yourself. If you have every thing done for
you, it will make you helpless. It is much better for
you to learn to help yourself; and women that do work
in a family do not like to wait on children who are
able to wait on themselves. Indeed, you ought to
make it a rule never to ask any one to do that for you

which you can do yourself. If you make yourself dependent upon others, you will be troublesome wherever you go, and an unwelcome guest among your friends. But do not be very familiar with hired men or women, nor make them your companions or confidants, for they may lead you astray.

In conclusion, I will give you one little *family rule*. You may think it a *very little* one; but it is able to do wonders. If you will try it one week, and never deviate from it, I will promise you the happiest week you ever enjoyed. And more than this, you will diffuse such a sunshine about you, as to make others happy also. My little rule is this: NEVER BE CROSS.

Illustrations.

SISTERLY AFFECTION.

Next to the duty of children to their parents is their duty to their brothers and sisters, of the same family. Affection lies at the foundation of the social relations, and mutual love is the reigning spirit in every well-regulated family. But love may exist, and yet sometimes give way to a naughty temper, the evils of which cannot, for a long time, be remedied. And, if you would cherish love, you must not do violence to it, by the indulgence of contrary feelings and dispositions. Love is a *tender plant*, which will not bear the *east wind*. The following anecdotes illustrate *both sides* of this subject.

THE MISS SINGERS.

The following account was given by Miss Philomela Singer, (afterwards Mrs. Rowe) to Rev. Dr. Colman. when he was in England:

"My sister was a year or two younger than I; and her affection, as well as wit, was quicker. I seemed, however, myself to think more thoroughly. She desired ever to be with me, and I wanted to be more by myself. We often retired, by consent, each to her chamber, to compose; and then meet to compare what we had written. She always exceeded me in the number of lines; but mine, I think, were more correct She exceeded me much in the fondness of love, but never in the truth and strength of it. She was jealous of me, that my love was not equal to hers, and invented a hundred ways to try me; many of which I thought childish and weak, and therefore sometimes rather reproved than complied with them. This gave her grief, and I found her in tears, which I could not put a stop to, but by the tenderest words and embraces.

"We lived years together, as happy as children could be in each other. We lived *religiously* together. We took care of one another's souls, and had our constant hours of retirement and devotion. We were daily speaking to each other of God; his being, perfections, and works; the wonders of creation and providence, the mysteries of redemption and grace. My father, in his widowhood, took great delight in us, and cherished our love to God, and one another; but, like good Jacob, was fondest of the youngest, admiring all she said and did; and in her death he was to be tried. But it was *I* that was taken sick, to a very dangerous degree. When my physicians were giving me over, my sister came to me, drowned in tears, and, earnestly kissing me, besought me to tell her whether I was, through grace, prepared to die; whether my interest in Christ and title to heaven were comfortable and clear to me. For she was afraid I should die, and she could not part with me, only to go to Christ, which was far better. I earnestly looked upon her, and said, 'Why!

sister, do you think me dangerous? I must confess
to you, my distress would be great, if I thought my
dying hour were now coming on; for I have not that full
assurance of my interest in Christ, which I have always
begged of God I might have, before he should call me
hence.'

"No sooner had she heard me say this, than she
fell, as in agony, on her knees, by my bed, and in a
manner inexpressible for fervour and humility, she
begged of God, that, if her father must have the grief
of burying one of his children, it might be *herself;* for
through his free grace, and to the glory of it, she could
humbly profess before him, her assured hope of her
interest in his everlasting mercy, through Jesus Christ:
wherefore she could gladly and joyfully surrender herself to die, if it might please God to grant her sister
further space wherein to make her calling and election
sure. Having prayed thus, in a transport which was
surprising and astonishing to me, she kissed me, and
left the room, without giving me time or power to
answer a word. And, what is almost incredible to relate, from that moment I grew better, and recovered;
but she took to her bed, and died within a few days.
Conceive, if you can, how I was astonished by this
event of Providence, and overwhelmed with sorrow; and
my father with me. The load of grief upon me confined me to my chamber for more than six weeks. My
chief work was to consider the mind of God, in this his
mercy to me; that I might make it evident to myself,
that, indeed, in love to my soul, he had delivered me
from the pit of destruction. We durst not be incon-
solable, under a bereavement so circumstanced; yet my
mourning is always returning, with the remembrance
of a love stronger than death, and, bright like those of
the seraphim, those flames of love and devotion."

The death of the younger sister might, perhaps, be accounted for on natural principles, by the influence of a strong belief that her prayer would be answered, upon a lively imagination, and a nervous temperament. But the recovery of the other could hardly be so accounted for. It is the more reasonable to regard it as a direct answer to prayer; which is agreeable to Scripture, for the feelings which the younger sister manifested were such as God approves. It was Christ-like. "Hereby perceive we the love of God, because he laid down his life for us; and *we ought to lay down our lives for the brethren.*" It was disinterested love; and who can help admiring its strength and ardour?

This example of sisterly affection is worthy of being followed; all except the jealousy manifested by the younger sister, lest the elder's love should not equal her own. Their example in helping each other on their way to heaven, and in conversing on heavenly things, is worthy the imitation of all good sisters.

A GENEROUS SISTER.

When Rev. Mr. Knibb, the missionary, was teaching a school in Jamaica, a little boy had been guilty of profaneness; and Mr. Knibb was going to shut him up for some hours alone, after school. But the little boy's sister came to him, and begged to be shut up instead of her brother. To try her affection, he consented; and she cheerfully took the boy's place, while he was dismissed. But the teacher, having satisfied himself of her sincerity, dismissed her; when she said, " School-massa, me know it bad for curse; and if my broder ever do it 'gin, me bring him you for punish." On their way home, the little boy swore again, and she immediately brought him back to be shut up.

THE PRAYING SISTERS.

Two brothers left their mother and sisters, and went to a distant State. There they embraced some fatal religious errors, which were like to prove their ruin. They had two pious sisters, who no sooner heard of it, than they agreed with each other to spend half an hour every Saturday evening at sunset, separately, in prayer, for their brothers. The two brothers were awakened, and hopefully converted to God. While this incident furnishes a beautiful example of sisterly affection, it likewise affords encouragement to pray for our friends, in the most desperate circumstances. God is a hearer of prayer.

EFFECTS OF UNKINDNESS.

THE following story is taken from the 'Religious Magazine,' a work which was several years ago published in the city of Boston. It is well told, and true to the life, so that, contrary to my usual practice, I have inserted it entire, without writing it over. Do any of my gentle readers ever get into such an angry, cross, unkind mood as that exhibited by Clara? If so, I think they cannot read this affecting story, without resolving never again to indulge such a temper.

ONE morning, there was a little girl sitting on the door-steps of a pleasant cottage near the Common. She was thin and pale. Her head was resting upon her slender hand. There was a touching sadness in her sweet face, which the dull, heavy expression about her jet-black eyes did not destroy.

Her name was Helen. For several weeks she had seemed to be drooping, without any particular disease, inconstant in her attendance at school, and losing gradually her interest in all her former employments. Helen had one sister, Clara, a little older than herself, and several brothers. While she was most indisposed, they had expressed a great deal of sympathy, and tried to amuse her, and had willingly given up their own enjoyments to promote hers. But children will too often be selfish; and when Helen, for some days, appeared better, and was able to run about and amuse herself, they would forget how peculiarly sensitive she had become; and the cross words which they occasionally spoke, and the neglect with which they sometimes treated her, wounded her feelings, and caused her to shed many bitter tears as she lay awake on her little cot at night.

This day she seemed better; and it was something her sister had said to her just before, which gave that expression of sadness to her face, as she sat at the door of the cottage. Clara soon came to her again.

"Helen, mother says you must go to school to-day; so get up, come along and get ready, and not be moping there any longer."

"Did ma say so !" said Helen.

"Yes, she did," replied Clara. "You are well enough, I know, for you always say you are sick at school-time. Get your bonnet, for I shan't wait."

Helen got up slowly, and wiping with her apron the tear which had started in her eye, made preparations to obey her mother's command.

Now Clara had a very irritable disposition. She could not bear to have Helen receive any more attention or sympathy than herself; and unless she were really so sick as to *excite her fears,* she never would allow her to be sick at all. She was determined not to go to school alone this morning, and had persuaded her mother to make her sister go with her.

In a few moments they were both ready; but now a difficulty presented itself. The distance to school was so great that they seldom returned at noon. Their dinner had been packed for them in a large basket, which stood in the entry. Upon whom, now, should the task of carrying this devolve?

"Helen," said Clara, "I've carried the basket every day for a week; it is your turn now."

"But it is twice as heavy now," said Helen. "I can but just lift it."

"Well, I don't care," replied Clara. "I have got my geography and atlas to carry; so take it up, and come along, Miss Fudge. *I* shan't touch it."

Helen took up the basket, without saying another word, though it required all her little strength, and walked slowly behind her sister. She tried hard to keep from crying; but the tears would come as fast as she wiped them off. They walked on thus in silence for about a quarter of an hour. Clara felt too much ill humour to take the least notice of her sister. She knew she had done wrong, and felt uneasy, but was yet too proud to give up, and was determined to "hold out;" excusing herself by thinking, "Well, Helen is always saying she is sick, and making a great fuss. It is just good enough for her." When she had reached the half-way stone, she had half a mind not to let her rest there, as usual; but the habit was too strong to be easily broken, and she sat down sullenly to wait for Helen to come up.

This was a spot which few could have passed unnoticed. The broad flat stone was shaded by a beautiful weeping-willow, whose branches hung so low, that even little Maria could reach them by standing on tiptoe; and around the trunk of this tree ran a little brook, which came up just to this rustic seat, and then turned off into the next meadow. It would seem as if the beauty of this place must have charmed away the evil spirit which was raging in Clara's breast: but no! The cool shade brought no refreshment to those evil passions, and the little ripples which sparkled in the sunbeam did not, for one moment, divert her attention from her own cross feelings. As I said before, she sat sullenly, till Helen came up, and then began to scold her for being so slow.

"Why don't you come along faster, Helen? You will be late to school, and I don't care if you are: you deserve a good scolding, for acting so."

"Why, Clara, I am *very tired*, my head *does* ache, and this basket is very heavy. I do think you ought to carry it the rest of the way."

"Do give it to me, then," said Clara; and snatched it from her with such violence, that the cover came off. The apples rolled out and fell into the water, the gingerbread followed, and the pie rolled into the dirt. It has been truly said, "Anger is a short madness;" for how little reason have those who indulge in it! Helen was not to blame for the accident, but Clara did not stop to think of this. Vexed at having thus lost her dinner, she turned and gave her little sister a push, and then walked on as rapidly as possible. Oh! could she have foreseen the consequences of this rash act, could she have known the bitter anguish which it would afterwards cause her, worlds would not have tempted her to do it; but *Clara was angry.* Helen was seated just on the edge of the stone, and she fell into the water. It was not deep. She had waded there many a day with her shoes and stockings off, and she easily got out again; but it frightened her very much, and took away all her strength. She could not even call to her sister, or cry. A strange feeling came over her, such as she had never had before. She laid her head on the stone; closed her eyes, and thought she was going to die; and she wished her mother was there. Then she seemed to sleep for a few moments; but bye and bye she felt better, and getting up she took her empty basket, and walked on as fast as she was able towards school.

It was nearly half done when she arrived there; and, as she entered the room, all noticed her pale face and wet dress. She took her seat, and, placing her book before her, leaned her aching head upon her hand, and attempted to study, but in vain. She could not fix her attention at all. The strange feeling began to come over her once more: the letters all mingled together; the room grew dark; the shrill voice of the little child screaming its A B C in front of her desk, grew fainter and fainter: her head sunk upon her book, and she fell to the floor.

Fainting was so unusual in this school, that all was instantly confusion, and it was some minutes before the teacher could restore order. Helen was brought to the air; two of her companions were despatched for water; and none were allowed to remain near excepting Clara, who stood by, trembling from head to foot, and almost as white as the insensible object before her. Oh! what a moment of anguish was this! deep, bitter anguish! Her anger melted away at once, and she would almost have sacrificed her own life to have recalled the events of the morning. That was impossible. The future, however, was still before her; and she *determined* never again to indulge her temper, or be unkind to any one. If Helen *only* recovered, the future would be spent in atoning for her past unkindness. It seemed, for a short time, indeed, as if she would be called upon to fulfil these promises. Helen gradually grew better, and in about an hour was apparently as well as usual. It was judged best, however, for her to return home; and a farmer, who happened to pass in a new gig, very kindly offered to take her.

Clara could not play with the girls as usual: she could not study. Her heart was full, and she was very impatient to be once more by her sister's side.

O how eagerly she watched the sun in his slow progress round the school-house! and when at last he threw his slanting beams through the west window, she was the first to obey the joyful signal; and books, papers, pen and ink, instantly disappeared from her desk.

Clara did not linger on her way home. She even passed the half-way stone with no other notice than a deep sigh. She hurried to her sister's bed-side, impatient to show her the curiosities she had collected, and to make up, by every little attention, for her unkindness. Helen was asleep. Her face was no longer pale, but flushed with a burning fever. Her little hands were hot; and, as she tossed restlessly about on her pillow, she would mutter to herself, sometimes calling on her sister, to "stop, stop," and then again begging her not to throw her to the fishes.

Clara watched long in agony, for her to awake.

This she did at last; but it brought no relief to the distressed sister and friends. She did not know them, and continued to talk incoherently about the events of the morning. It was too much for Clara to bear. She retired to her own little room and lonely bed, and wept till she could weep no more.

By the first dawn of light she was at her sister's bedside; but there was no alteration. For three days Helen continued in this state. I would not, if I could, describe the agony of Clara as she heard herself thus called upon and deservedly reproached by the dear sufferer. Her punishment was, indeed, greater than she could bear. At the close of the third day, Helen gave signs of returning consciousness, inquired if the cold water which she drank would injure her, recognised her mother, and anxiously called for Clara. She had just stepped out, but was immediately told of this. Oh! how joyful was the summons! She hastened to her sister, who, as she approached, looked up and smiled. The feverish flush from her cheek was gone: she was almost deadly pale. By her own request, her head had been raised upon two or three pillows, and her little emaciated hands were folded over the white coverlid. Clara was entirely overcome, she could only weep; and as she stooped to kiss her sister's white lips, the child threw her arms around her neck, and drew her still nearer. It was a long embrace: then her arms moved convulsively, and fell motionless by her side: there were a few struggles, she gasped once or twice, and little Helen never breathed again.

Days, and weeks, and months, rolled on. Time had somewhat healed the wound which grief for the loss of an only sister had made; but it had not power to remove from Clara's heart the remembrance of her former unkindness which poisoned many an hour.

She never took her little basket of dinner, now so light, or in her solitary walk to school passed the half-way stone, without a deep sigh, and often a tear of bitter regret.

Children who *are* what Clara *was,* go now and be what Clara *is:* mild, amiable, obliging and pleasant to all.

LOVE TO BROTHERS.

A GENTLEMAN, walking on the Battery in the city of New York, as he passed a little girl, who was blithely rolling her hoop, said, "You are a nice little girl," to which she replied, patting her little brother on the head, "And he is a nice little boy, too." Here was delicate, disinterested feeling. This amiable little girl could not bear even to hear herself praised, while her little brother was overlooked.

A LOVING SISTER.

SOPHIA had one sister, older than herself, whom she most tenderly loved. If she had any nice things, such as the first ripe strawberry or peach or plum, or any thing that her sister relished, she would save it, and share it with her, because she delighted so much in seeing her pleased. It seemed to give her more satisfaction to please her sister than to enjoy any pleasure herself. Such was her disinterested affection, that her teacher, on one occasion, in order to reward her, put down her sister's name among a select few who were to go with her to a concert.

Another time, the girls in the boarding school which

they attended, were directed to have a piece of sewing done the next morning; and, as Sophia's sister was sometimes negligent of her task, she was threatened with punishment if she failed. This she dreaded very much; but her dilatory habits prevailed; and when Sophia had finished hers, her sister had not begun. It was now evening, and she had abandoned the task in despair, thinking it too late to have it finished. The girls were all playing in the garden, in great glee, when it was suddenly discovered that Sophia was not among them. This occasioned great excitement among the group; for she was a general favourite, as every one will be who acts from the same disinterested feeling. After searching the house over, she was at last discovered in an old out-house, with the door fastened, busily at work on her sister's task, that she might save her the dreaded punishment. She was a happy creature. No doubt, she had much more enjoyment in making others happy, than she could have had, if it had been her great aim to please herself. Truly, as our Saviour says, "It is more blessed to give than to receive." If you seek to please others, you will be sure to please yourself; for you cannot fail to enjoy the happiness which you impart to others.

CHAPTER VI.

BEHAVIOUR AT SCHOOL.

MOST of what I have said in the last two chapters will apply to your behaviour at school. When you go to school, your teachers take the place of your parents. To them, for the time being, your parents have delegated their authority. You are bound, therefore, to give to them the same reverence and obedience which are due to your parents. To disobey, or to dishonour them in any other way, is a breach of the fifth commandment, which, in its spirit, requires *subordination to lawful authority;* or, as the Catechism says, "The fifth commandment requireth the preserving the honour of, and performing the duties belonging to, every one, in their several places and relations, as superiors, inferiors, or equals." You ought, therefore, in the first place, to pay strict regard to every rule of the school, as a religious duty; and obey your teacher, in all things, with the same promptness and cheerfulness that you would obey your parents. You should be too careful of your own reputation to permit yourself to be reprimanded by your teacher. If you take up the resolution that you will be so diligent, faithful, and well-behaved, as never to be reproved, you will find it a very wholesome restraint, to keep you within

3   E

the bounds of propriety.   Be careful of the *honour* of
your teachers, remembering that, if you dishonour
them, you break God's holy commandment.   Never
call in question their arrangements; and never indulge
feelings of dissatisfaction.   Especially, never speak
slightingly or disrespectfully of them, nor of their
ways.   It does not become you to call in question their
arrangements, or their mode of teaching.   If you are
wiser than they, you had better not seek instruction
from them; but if not, then you should be satisfied
with the dictates of their superior wisdom.   Never
attempt to question their proceedings, nor to argue
with them, when they require you to do any thing.
Be very careful, also, not to carry home tales from
school, because such a practice tends to cultivate a disposition to tattle, and often leads to great mischief.
Yet, when your parents make inquiries, it is your duty
to answer them.

Be diligent in your studies, from *principle*, not from
a spirit of emulation.   Remember that you are placed
at school for your own benefit.   It is not for your
parents' advantage, nor for the benefit of your teachers,
that you are required to study; but for your own good.
Remember how much pains your parents take, to give
you this opportunity.   They give up your time, which
they have a right to employ for their own benefit, and
they expend money for the support of schools, that you
may have the opportunity of obtaining useful learning.
You are bound, therefore, to improve this opportunity
with great diligence.   You will not think it a task,
that you are compelled to study; but you will regard
it as a price[1] put into your hands to get wisdom.   It
is all for your own benefit.   In school hours, therefore
you should put away all thoughts of play, and all

[1] Prov. xvii, 16.

communication with other scholars, and give yourself strictly and closely to your studies.

But, I suppose you will find the most difficulty in regulating your conduct during the intervals of school hours, and on your way to and from school. When a great many young persons of your own age are together, there is a disposition to throw off restraint. I would not have you under such restraint as to avoid all relaxation and innocent hilarity; for these are necessary to keep your mind and body in a healthful condition. But you must be careful to do nothing inconsistent with propriety; nothing out of character for your sex. If you go to a school composed of both sexes, as most of our country schools are, it would be unbecoming in you to play with the boys, or to associate with them, any further than to engage in modest and sensible conversation, which will be improving and profitable both to them and to yourself. But the sports in which boys usually engage are improper for your sex; and for you to engage in rude, boisterous conversation and coarse jesting, such as ill-bred youth are wont to practise, would be highly unbecoming. You ought to carry out the rules of good breeding, in all your intercourse with your fellow-pupils. Be kind, courteous, affable, and obliging toward all. Treat them as your brothers and sisters, except to remain more reserved than you do at home, especially towards those of the other sex. You must not allow boys to be too familiar; but be modest, and keep them at a respectful distance. And if they are inclined to be rude and unmannerly, have nothing at all to say to them. Choose, for your recreations, those sports which are gentle and suited to your sex, not rough and roisterous. Be especially careful of your conduct on the way, to and from school. Make it a principle always to be at school in time, and never linger by the way, either going or coming, for this will destroy your habits of punctuality, and expose you to many bad influences. It is of the utmost consequence to be punctual at school hours. All the affairs of the school are deranged by tardiness; and you not only suffer loss in your recitations, but in your habits.

There is often much impropriety practised at the intervals of school hours, and on the way to and from school; and there is great danger that thoughtless girls will lose their delicacy, and have their principles undermined, before they are aware of it. A man was at work in a ship-yard, in company with other men, in the building of a vessel. He was preparing one of the planks for the bottom of the ship. "There," said he to his comrades, "is a worm-hole," as he planed off the rough outside of the plank. The workmen examined it, but concluded the hole was so small it could never do any injury. The plank was put in the vessel. Some years afterwards, as that ship was at sea, there came up a violent storm, and the ship sprung a leak. On examining the bottom, it was found that the water had for a long time soaked into a worm-hole, and rotted the wood for some distance around, till now, in the time of trial, when the waves beat furiously against the ship, it had suddenly given way. The men on board made every exertion to get her ashore, but were obliged to abandon her, and she sunk to rise no more. Many a girl has been ruined in consequence of a very slight deviation from propriety, which has led on to others of a more serious nature, till, at length, her principles have been corrupted, and in the hour of temptation they have given way, and she has sunk to rise no more! A sad warning to others to watch against the *beginnings of evil*. It is the "little foxes," as Solomon says, that "spoil the vines."[1]   The old foxes eat the grapes; but the little foxes, running on the tender parts of the vines, as they put forth to bud and blossom, spoil them before the fruit grows.   It is thus that the character is corrupted and secretly undermined, by little causes, in early life.   When a girl consents, in a single instance, to step beyond the bounds of propriety, she exposes herself to the most imminent danger of ruin.   The following rule, if adhered to, will save you from a multitude of evils, while out of your parents' sight: ALWAYS CONDUCT AS YOU WOULD IF YOU WERE UNDER THE EYE OF YOUR PARENTS, AND NEVER FORGET THE ONE EYE THAT IS ALWAYS UPON YOU.

[1] Song, ii, 15.

CHAPTER VII

DID it ever occur to you to inquire why all civilized people have their food prepared at particular hours, and all the family sit at table together? Why not have the food prepared, and placed where every one can go and eat whenever he pleases by himself? One great advantage of having a whole family sit together, and partake of their meals at the same time, is, that it brings them together in a social way every day. But for this, and the assembling of the family at prayers, they might not all meet at once for a long time. But eating together is a mark of friendship; and it tends to promote social feeling. In a well-regulated family, also, it is a means of great improvement, both of mind and manners. It is, in fact, a *school of good manners.* You will perceive, then, how very important it is, that your behaviour at table should always be regulated by the rules of propriety. If you acquire vulgar habits here, or practise rudeness, you will find it difficult to overcome them; and they will make you appear to great disadvantage.

I shall mention a few things to be observed at the table, by one who would maintain a character for good breeding. And, first of all, be not tardy in taking your place at the table. In a well-regulated family, the master of the family waits till all are seated before he asks a blessing. Suppose there are five persons at the table, and you hinder them all by your tardiness three minutes, you waste fifteen minutes of precious time. To those who set a proper value upon time, this is a great evil. There is no need of it; you may as easily be at your seat in time as too late. When called to a meal, never wait to finish what you are doing, but promptly leave it, and proceed to your place. Above all, do not delay till after the blessing, and so sit down to your food like a heathen.

The table is a place for easy, cheerful, social intercourse; but some children make it a place of noisy clamour. The younger members of the family should leave it for the parents (and guests, if there are any,) to take the lead in conversation. It does not appear well for a very young person to be forward and talkative at table. You should generally wait till you are spoken to; or if you wish to make an inquiry or a remark, do it in a modest, unassuming way, not raising your voice nor spinning out a story. And be especially careful not to interrupt any other person. Sensible people will get a very unfavourable impression concerning you, if they see you bold and talkative at table. Yet you should never appear inattentive to what others are saying. Be not so intent on discussing the contents of your plate as not to observe the movements of others, or to hear their conversation. Show your interest in what is said by occasional glances at the speaker; and by the expression of your countenance; but be not too anxious to put a word in yourself. Some children make themselves ridiculous, by always joining in, and making their remarks, when older persons are speaking, often giving a grave opinion of some matter about which they know nothing.

Be helpful to others, without staring at them, or neglecting your own plate. You may keep your eye on the movements around you, to pass a cup and saucer, to notice if any one near you needs helping, and to help any dish that is within your reach. By so doing, you may greatly relieve your father and mother, who must be very busy, if they help all the family. By cultivating a close observation, and studying to know and anticipate the wants of others, you will be able to do these things in a genteel and graceful manner, without appearing obtrusive or forward.

Study *propriety*. If asked what you will be helped to, do not answer in an indefinite manner, saying, you "have no choice;" for this will put the master of the house to the inconvenience of choosing for you. Do not wait, after you are asked, to determine what you will have, but answer promptly; and do not be particular in your choice. To be very particular in the choice of food is not agreeable to good breeding. Never ask for what is not on the table. Do not make remarks respecting the food; and avoid expressing your likes and dislikes of particular articles. One of your age should not appear to be an epicure. Show your praise of the food set before you, by the good nature and relish with which you partake of it; but do not eat so fast as to appear voracious. Never put on sour looks, nor turn up your nose at your food. This is unmannerly, and a serious affront to the mistress of the table. Be careful to use your knife and fork as other people do, and to know when to lay them down, and when to hold them in your hands. Be careful not to drop your food, nor to spill liquids on the cloth. Do not leave the table before the family withdraw from it, unless it is necessary;

and then, ask to be excused. Neither linger to finish your meal, after you perceive the rest have done.

Besides what I have mentioned, there are a great many nameless little things, that go to make up good manners at table, which you must learn by studying the rules of propriety, and observing the behaviour of others.

CHAPTER VIII.

BEHAVIOUR AT FAMILY WORSHIP.

ALL well-regulated Christian families are assembled, morning and evening, to worship God. Seeing we are dependent on him for all things, it is suitable and proper that we should daily acknowledge our dependence, by asking him for what we need, and thanking him for what we receive. That we should do this *as a family* is highly proper. But if it is our duty to worship God *as a family*, it is the duty of every one in particular. It is as much your duty as it is your father's. You must, therefore, not only make it a principle to be in your place punctually at the time, but to enter heartily into all the exercises. Some children and youth appear as if they had no interest in what is going on at this most interesting household service. But this is not only showing great disrespect to your parents, but great irreverence toward God. It will help you to right feelings, on these occasions, if you imagine Christ Jesus present in person. God is present spiritually, and in a peculiar manner, at such times, to bless the families that call on his name. When, therefore, the family are assembled for prayers, you should put away all vain or wandering thoughts. When the time arrives, and the family are assembled for devotion, seat yourself in a serious reverent manner; and if there should be a few moments' delay, do not engage in conversation, nor in reading newspapers, or any thing calculated to divert your mind; but direct your thoughts upward to God, and seek a preparation for his worship. Suffer not your mind to be occupied with any thing but the service before you. Let not your eyes wander about, to catch vagrant thoughts. Let not your hands be occupied with any thing to divert your attention or to disturb others. Have your Bible, and take your turn in reading. Be attentive and devout during the reading of God's holy word, endeavouring to apply it to your heart. If the family sing, enter into this sweet service, not only with your lips, but with your heart. When prayer is offered, place yourself in the attitude which is taken by your father and mother. If they kneel, kneel you also; do not sit nor recline, but stand upon your knees in a reverent posture. Shut your eyes and keep your heart. Let your heart embrace the words of the prayer, and make them your own. Remember that the devotional habits you form at the family altar, are the habits that will follow you to God's house, and probably adhere to you through life. And what can be more shocking than to see persons pretending to gentility, who do not know how to behave with propriety before the great God that made them! If you were in company, and should treat the person that invited you with as much indifference as you treat God by such conduct, you would be considered a very ill-bred person. He has invited you to come to his mercy-seat to converse with him, and to receive favours at his hand; and yet, by such conduct as I have named, you show no interest at all in the matter.

Family devotion, when rightly improved, is a very important means of grace. If you attend upon it seriously and reverently, you may hope that God will bless it to your soul. It tends, also, to tranquillize the feelings, and prepare you to engage in the duties of the day with serenity and cheerfulness

CHAPTER IX.

PRIVATE PRAYER.

I SUPPOSE, if my readers are the children of pious parents, they have been taught from their earliest recollection, to retire, morning and evening, to some secret place, to read their Bible alone, and engage in private prayer. This, in very early childhood, is often an interesting and affecting service. But when young people come to a certain age, if their hearts are not renewed, they are disposed to regard this as an irksome duty, and gradually to leave it off. They find the old adage, in the primer, true: "Praying will make thee leave sinning, and sinning will make thee leave praying."

It is a sad period, in the history of a young person, when the early habit of prayer is given up. Then the heart becomes like the garden of the slothful, described by Solomon:

"I went by the field of the slothful, and by the vineyard of the man void of understanding; and lo, it was all grown over with thorns, and nettles had covered the face thereof, and the stone wall thereof was broken down."

There are no good plants thriving in the prayerless

soul; but weeds, and briers, and thorns, grow thick and rank, occupying every vacant spot. The stone wall is broken down: there is no defence against the beasts of the field. Every vagrant thought, every vicious passion, find free admittance. The heart grows hard, and the spirit careless. Sin is not dreaded as it once was. The fear of God and the desire of his favour are gone. "God is not in all his thoughts." That youth stands on the very edge of a frightful precipice.

I would not have you think, however, that there is any *merit* in prayer; or that the prayers of one whose "heart is not right with God" are acceptable to him. But, what I say is, that every one ought to pray to God with a right heart. If your heart is not right with God, then it is wrong; and you are to blame for having it wrong. I will suppose a case, to illustrate what I mean. You see a child rise up in the morning, and go about the house; and though its mother is with it all the time, yet the child neither speaks to her nor seems to notice her at all. After a while, the mother asks what is the matter, and why her dear child does not speak to her? The child says, "I have *no heart* to speak to you, mother. I do not *love* you; and so I think it would be wrong for me to speak to you." What would you think of such conduct? You would say, "The child *ought* to love its mother; and it is only an aggravation of its offence, to carry out the feelings of its heart in its conduct?" Would you then have it act the hypocrite, and speak with its lips what it does not feel in its heart? No; but I would have it love its mother, as every dutiful child ought to do, and then act out, in its speech and behaviour, what it feels in its heart. But I would never have it excuse itself from right actions because its heart is wrong. Now, apply this to the subject of prayer, and you will see the

character of all impenitent excuses for neglecting this
duty. And those who go on and continue to neglect
it, certainly have no reason to expect that their hearts
will grow any better by it, but only worse. But in
attempting to perform a sacred duty, the Lord may
give you grace to perform it aright, and then you will
have a new heart.

If possible, have a particular place of prayer where
you can be secure from all interruption, and particular
times for it. At the appointed hours retire alone, and
put away all thoughts about your studies, your work,
your amusements, or any thing of a wordly nature, and
try to realize that God is as truly present as if you saw
him with your bodily eyes. Then read his word, as
though you heard him speaking to you in the sacred
page; and when your mind has become serious and
collected, kneel down and acknowledge God as your
Creator and Preserver, your God and Redeemer; thank
him for the mercies you have received, mentioning
particularly every good thing you can think of, that
you have received from him; confess your sins; plead
for pardon, through the blood of Jesus Christ; and ask
him to give you such blessings as you see and feel that
you need. Pray also for your friends, (and for your
enemies, if you have any;) and conclude with a prayer
for the coming of Christ's kingdom every where
throughout the world.

Some young people neglect to pray, because they
think they are not able to form their words into prayer.
But you need not be afraid to speak to God. If you
can find language to ask your parents for what you
desire, you can find words to express your desires to
God; and he will not upbraid you for the imperfection
of your language. He looks at the heart. If that is
right, your prayer will be accepted.

Let me earnestly entreat you to have your set times for prayer, at least as often as morning and evening; and never suffer yourself to neglect them. And, especially, do not adopt the unseemly practice of saying your prayers in bed, but give to God the brightest and best hours of the day, and offer not to him the blind and the lame for sacrifice. You will find the regular and stated habit of prayer thus formed in early life, of great value to you as long as you live.

But let me once more caution you not to trust in your prayers, for they cannot save you; and do not think because you are regular and habitual in attending to the outward forms of duty, that you must be a Christian.

Prayer, if sincere and true, will prepare you for engaging in the duties of the day, or for enjoying calm repose at night. If, for any cause, you neglect prayer in the morning, you may expect things will go ill with you all the day. You can do nothing well without God's blessing; and you cannot expect his blessing without asking for it. You need, also, that calm, tranquil, humble spirit which prayer promotes, to prepare you to encounter those things which are constantly occurring to try the feelings, and to enable you to do any thing well. Therefore, never engage in any thing of importance without first seeking direction of God; and never do any thing on which you would be unwilling to ask His blessing.

Illustrations.

PRAYING IN SECRET.

LITTLE Mary W. was asked, "Which do you love best, to pray in the family, or in secret?" Her reply was, "I love to pray with others; but I can say to God when I am alone, what I cannot say when I am with others."

A little girl in the country was frequently sent to a spring, some distance from the house, for water. Her father noticed that she sometimes stayed longer than was necessary, and one day followed her without being noticed. When she got to the spring, she set down her pitcher and kneeled down to pray. When she arose, he came forward and said, "Well, my dear, was the water sweet?" "Yes, father," she replied, "and if you were but to taste one drop of the water I have been tasting, you would never drink the water of this world any more."

PRAY WITHOUT CEASING.

AT a ministers' meeting, the question was proposed, "How can the command *'Pray without ceasing'* be

3   F

complied with?" After some discussion, one was appointed to write upon it for the next monthly meeting. A female servant, overhearing the conversation, exclaimed, "What! a whole month wanted to explain the meaning of that text! It is one of the easiest and best texts in the Bible." "Well, well," said an aged minister, "Mary, what can you say about it? Let us know how you understand it. Can you pray all the time?" "O yes, sir," she answered. "What, when you have so many things to do?" "Why, sir, the more I have to do, the more I can pray." "Indeed; well, Mary, do let us know how it is; for most people think otherwise." "Well, sir," said the girl, "When I first open my eyes in the morning, I pray, 'Lord, open the eyes of my understanding;' and while I am dressing, I pray that I may be clothed with the robe of righteousness; and when I have washed myself, I ask for the washing of regeneration; and as I begin to work, I pray that I may have strength equal to my day. When I begin to kindle the fire, I pray that God's work may revive in my soul; and as I sweep the house, I pray that my heart may be cleansed from all its impurities. While preparing and partaking of breakfast, I desire to be fed with the hidden manna, and the sincere milk of the word; and as I am busy with the little children, I look up to God as my father, and pray for the Spirit of adoption, that I may be his child. And so on, all day, every thing I do furnishes me with a thought for prayer." "Enough, enough," cried the aged minister; "these things are revealed to babes, though often hid from the wise and prudent. Go on, Mary, pray without ceasing; and as for us my brethren, let us thank God for this exposition, and remember that He has said, 'The meek will he guide in judgment.'" It is not to be supposed that these ministers were ignorant of the meaning of this text; but it must have been gratifying to them to see how Christian experience will exemplify it, so as to render any explanation unnecessary. If our readers will follow the example of this servant-girl, they will learn how to "be in the fear of God all the day long."

CHAPTER X.

SOME people esteem it a hardship to be compelled to keep the Sabbath. They think it an interference with their liberties, that the State should make laws to punish them for breaking it. This disposition very early shows itself in children. Often they think it is hard that they are restrained from play, or from seeking their pleasure, on the holy Sabbath. But God did not give us the Sabbath for his own sake, or because he is benefited by our keeping it. The Bible says, "The Sabbath was made for man." God gave us the Sabbath for our benefit, and for two purposes. He has made us so that we need rest one day in seven. It has been proved, upon fair trial, that men cannot do as much, nor preserve their health as well, by labouring seven days in a week, as they can by labouring six days, and resting one day in a week. If there were no Sabbath, you would have no day of rest. You would grow weary of school, if you were obliged to attend and study seven days in a week. If you are kept at home to work, you would soon tire out if you had to labour every day in the week. But by resting every seventh day, you get recruited, so that you are able to go on with study or work with new vigour. The Sabbath, in this respect, is then a great blessing to you; and you ought to be so thankful to God for it, as to keep it strictly according to his command.

Another object of the Sabbath is, to give all people an opportunity to lay aside their worldly cares and business, to worship God and learn his will. The other design of the Sabbath was, to *benefit the body;* this is, to *bless the soul.* If there were no Sabbath, people that are dependent upon others would be obliged to work every day in the week; and they would have no time to meet together for the worship of God. And, if every one were allowed to choose his own time for worshipping God, there would be no agreement. One would be at meeting, another would be at work, and others would be seeking their pleasure. But, in order to have every one at liberty to worship God without disturbance, he has set apart one day in seven for this purpose. On this day, he requires us to rest from all labour and recreation, and spend its sacred hours in learning his will, and in acts of devotion. The Sabbath thus becomes a means of improving the mind and the heart. It furnishes the best opportunity for social improvement that could be devised. It brings the people together in their best attire, to exercise their minds in understanding divine truth, and their hearts in obeying it. And the same object and the same spirit it carries out in a family. If, therefore, you ever consider the duties of the holy Sabbath irksome and unpleasant, or feel uneasy under its restraints, you perceive that you must be very unreasonable, since they are designed for your good. You will not then find fault with me, if I am rigid in requiring the strict observance of the Sabbath. One thing I would have you remember: *If you would receive the full benefit of the holy Sabbath, you must form right habits of keeping it early in life.* To give it full power over the mind, it must be associated in our earliest recollections, with order, quiet, stillness, and solemnity. If you are in the habit of disregarding it in early life, you lose all the benefit and enjoyment to be derived from these sacred associations.

The best directions for keeping the Sabbath any where to be found, are contained in the thirteenth verse of the fifty-eighth chapter of Isaiah: "If thou turn away thy foot from the Sabbath from doing thy pleasure on my holy day, and call the Sabbath a delight, the holy of the Lord, honourable; and shalt honour him, not doing thine own ways, nor finding thine own pleasure, nor speaking thine own words." You must *turn away your foot from the Sabbath,* not trampling on it by doing your own pleasure, instead of the pleasure of the Lord. Your foot must not move to perform any act that is contrary to the design of this sacred day; and especially, must not go after your own pleasure. You must not *do your own ways,* nor *find your own pleasure.* These things may be lawful on other days; but on this day, every thing must have reference to God. You must not even *speak your own words.* Worldly, vain, light, or trifling conversation is thus forbidden. And if you may not speak your own words, you may not think your own thoughts. Worldly, vain, trifling thoughts, or thoughts of your pleasure, are not lawful on God's holy day. But you must not only *refrain* from these things; the Sabbath is not properly kept, unless its sacred services are a *delight* to the soul. If you are tired of hearing, reading, and thinking of the things of another world, you do not keep the Sabbath according to these directions.

To one who enters truly into the spirit of God's holy day, it is the most delightful of the seven. You remember, in the memoir of Phebe Bartlett it is stated, that she so loved the Sabbath that she would long to have it come, and count the days intervening before it. Such are the feelings of all who love God and sacred things.

Having made these general remarks, I will give you a few simple directions for making the Sabbath both profitable and delightful. The evening before the Sabbath, do every thing that can be done, to save doing on the Sabbath. Leave nothing to be done in *God's time* that you can do in your *own time.* Lay out your Sabbath day's clothing, and see that it is all in order, that you may have no brushing or mending to be done on Sabbath morning. Rise early in the morning, and, while washing and dressing, which you will do in as little time as possible, think of your need of the "washing of regeneration and renewing of the Holy Ghost," and of being clothed in the clean, white robe of Christ's righteousness. Then offer up your thanksgiving to God for his mercy in preserving your life, and giving you another holy Sabbath, and pray for his presence and blessing through the day. If you are called by your father or mother, for any service of the family, go to it cheerfully; and as soon as you can retire again, read a portion of Scripture, and pray to God for such particular blessings upon yourself as you feel your need of, and for his blessing upon others on his holy day. If you attend the Sabbath school, you will need to look over your lesson for the day, and endeavour to apply it to your own heart; for I suppose you do not put off the study of your lesson till Sabbath morning.

Never stay at home on the Sabbath, unless you are

necessarily detained. Make it a matter of principle and calculation always to be there. On your way to the house of God, do not engage in any unnecessary conversation, especially that which is vain, light, or trifling, to divert your mind, and unfit you for the worship of God. Do not stand about the doors of the meeting-house, to salute your friends, or to converse with your young companions. This practice, I am sorry to say, prevails in the country, among young people of both sexes, to the great annoyance of well-bred people. It is a great temptation to conversation improper for the Sabbath. It is very unpleasant for people who are passing, to have the way blocked up, so as to have to press through a crowd. Neither do people like to be *stared at*, by a company of rude young people, as they pass into the house of God. I am sorry to admit, also, that this unmannerly practice is not confined to youth; but that many elderly people set the example. Instead of doing so, go directly to your seat, in a quiet, reverent manner; and if any time intervenes before the commencement of public worship, do not spend it in gazing about the house, to observe the dress of different persons; but take the opportunity to compose your mind, to call in all vagrant thoughts, to get your heart impressed with a sense of God's presence, and to lift up your soul in silent prayer for his blessing. Or, if the time be long, you can employ a part of it in reading the Bible, or devotional hymns. But do not carry any other book to the house of worship to be read there. If you have a Sabbath school library book, it will be better not to read it at such a time, because you will be likely to get your mind filled with it, so as to interfere with the services of the sanctuary. But the Bible and hymn book, being of a devotional character, will tend to prepare your mind for worship. Above all, do not read a newspaper, of any kind, at such a time. Even a religious newspaper would tend to divert your mind from that serious, tender, devout frame, which you ought to possess when you engage in the solemn public worship of the Great Jehovah. But I have often witnessed more serious improprieties, in the house of God, than any of these. I have seen young people whispering and laughing during the sermon; and it is a very common thing to see them gazing about during the singing, as though they had nothing to do with the service. I have also seen them engaged in reading, in the time of sermon, or of singing. Some, also, are seen, in time of prayer, with their eyes wide open, gazing about. Such conduct would be very unmannerly, if nobody were concerned but the minister; for it is treating him as though he were not worthy of your attention. But when it is considered that he speaks to you *in the name of God*, and that, in prayer, while you stand up with the congregation, you profess to join in the prayer; and while the hymn is sung, you profess to exercise the devout feeling which it expresses: when all these things are considered, such conduct as that I have described appears impious in a high degree.

Instead of being guilty of such improprieties, you will endeavour from the heart to join in the sentiments expressed in prayer and praise; and listen to the sermon with all attention, as a message sent from God to you. You must not think that the sermon is designed for older people, and therefore you have nothing to do with it; nor take up the notion that sermons are too dry and uninteresting to engage your attention. The minister speaks *to you*, in the name of God, those great truths which concern the salvation of the soul. Can they be of no interest to you? Have you not a soul to be saved or lost? Nor need you think that you cannot understand the sermon. If you *give your attention*, you can understand a sermon as well as you can understand the lessons you are required every day to study at school. If you do not understand preaching, it is because you do not give your mind to it, and hear with attention. Your mind is here and there, "walking to and fro in the earth and going up and down in it;" and you only catch, here and there, a sentence of the sermon. This is the reason you do not understand it. Endeavour to examine your heart and life by what you hear, and to apply it to yourself in such a way as to be benefited by it. And, when you leave the house of God, do not immediately engage in conversation, and by this means dissipate all impression; but, as far as possible, go home in silence, and retire to your closet, to seek the blessing of God upon the services of his house, on which you have attended.

I suppose, of course, that you attend the Sabbath school. I think it a great advantage to those who rightly improve it. But like every other privilege, it may be so neglected or abused as to be of no benefit. If you pay no attention to the Sabbath school lesson at home, your mere attendance upon the recitation at school will do you little good. You will feel little interest and receive little profit. But if you make it the occasion for the faithful study of the Holy Scriptures at home to ascertain their meaning, and to become acquainted with the great truths of Christianity, it will be of great service to you in forming your Christian character.

Having well and thoroughly studied your Sabbath school lesson, you will then be prepared to engage in the recitation with interest. In the Sabbath school you will observe the same general directions for propriety of behaviour as in public worship. You are to remember that it is the holy Sabbath, and that the Sabbath school is a religious meeting. All lightness of manner is out of place. A serious deportment is necessary, if you would profit by it. Courtesy to your teacher, and to the school, also requires that you should give your attention, and not be conversing or reading during the recitation, or while your teacher is speaking to you. In answering the questions you should be full and explicit; not merely making the briefest possible reply, but entering into the subject with interest. But be careful that you do not give indulgence to a self-confident, conceited spirit, nor appear as if you thought yourself wiser than your teacher. Such a spirit indulged will have an injurious influence in the formation of your character, and will make you an object of disgust to sensible people.

Some young people, when a little past the period of childhood, begin to feel as if they were too old to attend the Sabbath school, and so gradually absent themselves, and finally leave it altogether. This arises from a mistaken notion as to the design of the Sabbath school. It is not a school *for children merely;* but a school for all classes of people to engage in the study of the most wonderful book in the world. I hope you will never think of leaving the Sabbath school as long as you are able to attend it. If you do, you will suffer a loss which you will regret as long as you live.

If you remain at the house of worship between the Sabbath school and the afternoon service, as many do in the country, you will be exposed to temptations to profane the Sabbath. To prevent this, avoid meeting with your companions, in groups, for conversation

However well-disposed you may be, you can hardly avoid being drawn into conversation unsuitable for the holy Sabbath. If you take a book from the Sabbath school library, this will be a suitable time to read it, if you are careful not to extend the reading into the afternoon service, or suffer your thoughts to be diverted by what you have read. But the practice of reading the Sabbath school books during divine service, which prevails among children, and even with some young men and women, is not only very irreverent, but a gross violation of good breeding. It is slighting the service of God, and treating the minister as though they thought what he has to say to them not worth their attention.

You ought to have a particular time set apart for the study of your Sabbath school lesson. I should prefer that this be taken during the week; so as not to task your mind too severely on the Sabbath with *study*, inasmuch as it is a day of *rest*. But, if you cannot do this, I should advise that you study it on Sabbath afternoon, and review it the next Sabbath morning.

Some portion of the Sabbath afternoon, or evening, you will employ, under the direction of your parents, in repeating the Catechism, which I hope none of my readers will consider beneath their attention. '*The Shorter Catechism*,' next to the Bible, I regard as the best book in existence to lay the foundation of a strong and solid religious character. If you get it thoroughly committed to memory, so as to be able to repeat it verbatim from beginning to end, you will never regret it; but, as long as you live, you will have occasion to rejoice in it. I cannot now give you any adequate idea of the benefit you will derive from it. These catechetical exercises in your father's house will be associated in your mind with the most precious recollections of your early years. As I said with regard to your Sabbath school lessons, and for the same reason, I should advise you, if possible, to study the portion of the Catechism to be recited during the week. But if you cannot do so, it should be studied on the afternoon or evening of the Sabbath. If, however, you study these lessons in the week time, you will be able to spend the afternoon and evening of the Sabbath, except what is devoted to family worship and repeating the Catechism, in reading serious and devotional books, which will not tax your mind so much. If you are engaged in study all the week, your mind will need rest. Therefore, I would have you prosecute your *religious study* during the week, and let your mind be taxed less on the Sabbath, reading such books and engaging in such services as are calculated more to affect the heart than to tax the mind. You ought to spend more time than usual on God's holy day in your closet, in reading the Scriptures, and prayer. But besides the Bible, I would particularly recommend religious biographies, and such works as Bunyan's 'Pilgrim's Progress' and 'Holy War,' D'Aubigne's 'History of the Reformation,' and similar works. But secular history, or any books or papers of a secular character, should not be read on the holy Sabbath. In general, you may safely read on Sabbath afternoon the books that you find in the Sabbath school library; though it will sometimes happen that a book creeps into the library that is not suitable for this sacred day. A portion of the evening of the Sabbath, before retiring to rest, should be spent in reviewing the day, recollecting the sermons, examining how you have kept the day, and seeking in prayer the pardon of what has been amiss, and God's blessing on all the services in which you have been engaged.

A Sabbath thus spent will be a blessing to you, not only for the six days following, but as long as you live. It will contribute to the formation of religious habits that you will be thankful for to the day of your death. And when you become accustomed to spending your Sabbaths thus, so far from finding them long and tedious days, you will find them the most delightful of the seven, and will only regret that they are TOO SHORT: they come to an end before you have finished all the good designs you have formed.

Illustrations.

THE JEWS.

THE fact that God has set apart a day to himself, and commanded us to keep it holy, would naturally lead us to conclude that he would order his Providence so as to favour its observance. We have only need to examine the subject to be convinced that he does so. When his ancient people, the children of Israel, refused to keep his Sabbaths, and trampled his holy day under foot, he emptied them out of the land, and caused them to be carried off into a strange country, and to remain there seventy years. This was threatened in Leviticus, xxvi, 34, 35: "Then shall the land enjoy her Sabbaths, as long as it lieth desolate, and ye be in your enemies' land; even then shall the land rest, and enjoy her Sabbaths. As long as it lieth desolate, it shall rest; because it did not rest in your Sabbaths, when ye dwelt upon it." In 2 Chron. xxxvi, 20, 21, this is referred to as one of the principal reasons why they were carried away to Babylon: "And them that escaped the sword carried he away to Babylon; where they were servants to him and his sons, until the reign of the kingdom of Persia, to fulfil

the word of the Lord by the mouth of Jeremiah the
prophet, until the land had enjoyed her Sabbaths; for
as long as she lay desolate, she kept Sabbath, to fulfil
threescore and ten years."

GOD PUNISHES SABBATH-BREAKERS.

I CAN think of no reason why God, in his holy
Providence, should not punish Sabbath-breakers now
as well as then. I have no doubt that he does. If
we could see the design of his Providence, as it is
explained in the Bible, no one would doubt it. Sir
Matthew Hale, after a long and laborious public life,
declared, as the result of his experience, that he found
his affairs prosper, during the week, just in proportion
to the strictness with which he had observed the Sabbath; and that he had never met with success in any
business which was planned on the Sabbath.

I might fill this book with narratives of accidents
that have happened to young people, while seeking
their pleasure on the Lord's day. Scarcely a week
occurs, in the summer season, but the papers contain
accounts of parties of young people drowned while
taking Sabbath excursions on the water, or of young
men and boys drowned while bathing on the Lord's day.
Many very striking accounts of this kind have been collected and published in tracts. And a great many facts of
a more general nature have also been published, in various
forms, showing that it is *profitable* to keep the Sabbath,
and *unprofitable* and dangerous to break it. My object
in this place, is simply to impress on the minds of my
readers the very important influence which the proper
observance of the Sabbath has in the *formation of
character*. And I wish them to follow the youth through

life who has been accustomed to keep the Sabbath, and who continues to keep it; and then follow the course of one who has, in early life, been accustomed to disregard God's holy day. And one thought, in particular, I desire you to ponder well: *The Sabbath-breaker cannot expect God's protection.* And, if God forsakes you, what will become of you?

A party of young people set out for a sail on the Sabbath day. One of the young ladies told her brother that she felt very bad to think she was breaking the Sabbath, and she must return home. But he entreated her not to spoil his pleasure, for he should not enjoy it, unless she went with him; and to please him she consented to go. The boat was upset, and she was drowned. The distracted brother now gave vent to his grief in the most bitter lamentation. He had been the means of her death. There he stood, wringing his hands in agony, and exclaiming, " O! what shall I do! How can I see my father's face!"

A MELANCHOLY EXAMPLE.

SOME years ago, a young lady in New York went out on Sabbath morning, as her mother supposed, to go to meeting. Indeed, I believe she told her mother that she was going to church. I think it most likely, from the story as it appeared in the papers at the time, that she started with the intention of going to the house of God. She was seen on the sidewalk, speaking with a young man. It was not known what conversation passed between them; but it was supposed, from what followed, that he was an acquaintance of hers, and was inviting her to an excursion to Hoboken, a place of great resort for pleasure near New York, on the opposite side of the river. Very little is known of the manner in which she spent the day. Probably, they first had a sail for pleasure on the river, and afterwards promenaded the beautiful walks and delightful groves of Hoboken. She was seen in the afternoon, in company with some young men, at a public house of low character at Hoboken. Her body was found, the next day, at some distance from the house. She had been shamefully abused and murdered.

This melancholy case affords a striking illustration of the single point that I desire strongly to impress on your mind: GOD WILL NOT PROTECT THE SABBATH-BREAKER. When we trample on his holy day, he leaves us to ourselves. And what can we do without his protection? If he forsakes us, who can save us from destruction? This case shows, also, the great danger to which girls or young ladies expose themselves when they smother the voice of conscience, and consent to go with a company of Sabbath-breakers, in pursuit of pleasure, on God's holy day. The young man, who has so hardened his heart as openly to trample on the fourth commandment, will not scruple to violate any other of God's commands, when temptation and opportunity present themselves. It was so in this case. The young men in whose company this young lady intrusted herself were a band of Sabbath-breakers. You see what they did in the end. If you consent to put yourself in the power of boys or young men who will violate the Sabbath, and put yourself out of God's protection, by violating it yourself, you cannot expect any better result.

CHAPTER XI.

HABITS.

BESIDES what I have noticed in several of the foregoing chapters, there are many things of a general nature which I shall group together under the title of *habits*. A *habit* is what has become easy and natural by frequent repetition. People not unfrequently become much attached to practices, which at first were very unpleasant. You will sometimes see men chewing, smoking, or snuffing *tobacco*, a most filthy and poisonous plant, a little bit of which you could not be persuaded to take into your mouth, it is so nauseous; yet by long use people learn to love it. That is a *habit*. So, likewise, you see persons very fond of drinking intoxicating liquors, which to you would be a nauseous medicine, and which are poisonous and destructive to all. It is *practice* which has made these drinks so pleasant. This is a *habit*.

Habits are both *bad* and *good;* and a habit is a very good or a very bad thing, as it is good or bad. Habits are mostly formed in early life; and a habit once formed is difficult to be broken; once fixed, it may follow you as long as you live.

I shall specify a few of the bad habits which girls of your age sometimes contract, with their opposite good habits. It is very likely I shall fail to notice many others, equally important; but these may put you upon thinking, and lead you to discover and correct other bad practices.

I. DILATORINESS, or TARDINESS. The tardy girl is dilatory about rising in the morning. Although old Chanticleer is pouring his shrill note of warning into her ear, and the birds are filling the air with their merry song, and the morning rays of the sun are peeping stealthily through the half-closed shutter, still she thinks, "*There's time enough yet;*" and, instead of starting up with the lark, she lingers and delays. She rises in a yawning mood, and slowly and tardily proceeds to adjust her dress, lingering with every article, perhaps stopping to view it in some point which she had not noticed before; or she casts her eye on a piece of an old newspaper, and stops to read that; or her attention is attracted by something on the wall; she stands a long time at the glass, fixing her hair, or adjusting her curls; and thus the time is frittered away till the breakfast bell rings, and she is not ready. Her mother and the hired girl have been up an hour and a half; and perhaps she has been called three or four times, and as often answered, "*Well, I'm coming.*" At length she makes her appearance at the table after the blessing, when the rest of the family have begun their meal. Or, if she gets dressed before breakfast time, she is not in season to render the assistance to her mother which she needs, or to complete the lesson, which, through her tardiness, she left unfinished the evening before. She hears the bell, but she is just now engaged, and thinks "*There's time enough yet, I'll just finish what I've begun;*" and so she is not in season at the table. She has either detained the table till all are impatient of waiting, or else she takes her seat after the rest have commenced eating. But she is so dilatory in preparing her food, that she is hardly ready to begin till the rest have half finished their meal. She is left at the table to finish her breakfast, and her seat is for some time vacant at prayers, when she comes in and disturbs the whole family. This dilatoriness goes on till the school hour arrives, and she is not ready. At five or ten minutes past nine, she seizes her satchel, and hastens to school, where she arrives, out of breath, just after her class has recited. On Sabbath morning, when the bell tolls and the family start for meeting, they are detained at the door to wait for her; she has neglected to find her muff, her gloves, or her Sabbath school book, and she must stop and look it up. Thus it is in all things. When her mother calls her, instead of promptly coming to her assistance, it is, " *Yes, in a minute,*" or, " *Yes, I'm going to.*" She must dispose of something else first. She does not seem to know how to start quick. She is always in a hurry when the time comes to do any thing, because she was dilatory in making preparation when she had time. She is always late, always out of time, vexing those that are about her, and injuring herself. She always seems to have *started too late.* You would think she began too late in the beginning, that she was *born too late,* and so always keeps behindhand. Every thing comes *too soon,* before she is prepared for it. She will probably keep her wedding party waiting half an hour after the time set, before she will be ready for the ceremony. It is greatly to be feared that she will carry this dilatory habit into religion, and that *death* will overtake her *before she is ready.*

Although all this seems *natural* to her, yet it is only tardiness indulged till it has grown into a habit. It has become a sort of *second nature.* But by resolution, diligence, and perseverance, the habit may be broken.

The opposites of this are the good habits of PROMPT-NESS AND PUNCTUALITY. The prompt girl will rise with the lark in the morning. When the grey dawn steals in at her window, she springs from her bed, and in a very few minutes she is dressed, and prepared to make her appearance in the family, to assist her mother, if necessary, or, if not needed there, to go to her devotions and her study. She has done, perhaps, in fifteen or twenty minutes, what the dilatory girl would be an hour and a half in doing, and done it equally well. She is *always in time*. Her promptness enables her to be punctual. She never keeps the table waiting for her, and never comes after the blessing. She is never late at prayers; never late at school; never late at meeting; and yet she is never in a hurry. She redeems so much time by her promptness, that she has as much as she needs to do every thing well and in time. She saves all the time that the dilatory spends in sauntering, in considering what to do next, in reading frivolous matters, and in gazing idly at vacancy. Do you desire to possess these good habits? Only carry out the idea I have given of promptness one day, and then repeat it every day, and, in a little time, you have the habit established.

II. UNTIDINESS. An untidy girl leaves her things scattered about her room. She never has a place for any thing; or if she has, she does not keep any thing in it. She leaves a thing where she uses it. Her room is all confusion. If she wants any thing, she never knows where it is, but must hunt till she finds it, which costs her a great deal more precious time than it would have done to have put it in its proper place. If she goes into another person's room, whatever article she lays her hand upon is misplaced. She never thinks of putting it where she found it; but either throws it carelessly down, or puts it in the wrong place. If she goes to the library, and takes down a book, she either puts it up in a different place, and thus disarranges the shelves, or she lays it down on the shelf in front of other books, for her father or mother to arrange. If she carries a book from the library to read, she leaves it wherever she happens to be when she stops reading; and, perhaps, lays it down open upon its face, soiling its leaves, and straining it out of shape. And the next time she comes that way, if she happens to want to open the window, she will take the same book, without any regard to its value, and put it under the window. By this time, she has let it fall half a dozen times on the floor, bruising its nice binding, and loosening the leaves. And all the while she is reading, her fingers are busily employed in crumpling the leaves. Thus, by the time the book gets back to the library, it is in a worse condition than it would have been in two years with careful handling. Her school books are torn and dirty; disfigured with pencil marks, blots of ink, grease spots, finger prints, and dog's-ears; and if she borrows a book from the library, or of a friend, it is returned with some of these *her marks* upon it.

If she goes into the kitchen, she is sure to put the tidy housekeeper in a passion, for whatever she lays her hand upon is out of place. Nor does her own person appear to any better advantage. Her dress is adjusted in bad taste; it seems to hang out of shape. You would say her garments were *flung* upon her; and you feel an involuntary anxiety lest they should *fall off*. You do not perceive precisely what is the matter, but there is an evident want of neatness and taste. Her hair wears the same air of negligence; her face often discovers the lack of soap, and her finger nails want attention.

These are only a few examples of the effects of

untidy habits. When untidiness becomes a habit, it
runs through every thing. And the untidy girl will
make an untidy woman; and the untidy woman will
make an untidy house; and an untidy house will spoil
a good husband. A man of taste cannot enjoy himself where every thing is out of order; and he will seek
that pleasure abroad which he finds not at home.

The twin sister of untidiness is CARELESSNESS. The
careless girl is always unfortunate. If she goes into
the kitchen, to assist about the work, she splashes
water on the wall, drops oil on the floor, spills fat in
the fire, scorches her clothes, burns her biscuit, breaks
the crockery, or cuts her finger with the carving-knife.

If directed to sweep the family room, she oversets a
lamp, or brushes off a table cover, and sends Bibles and
hymn-books sprawling on the floor; or if passing through
the parlour, she swings her dress against the centre-
table, and brushes off the costly books, bruising their
fancy binding, and soiling their gilt edges. Every
where she goes, something is found in ruins. The
trouble is, she *does not think*, she does not *observe;* or
else her thoughts and observations are on something
besides what is before her. She does not mind what
she is doing. She does not look to see what she steps
on, nor whether her hands have firm hold of the article
which she takes up. If she passes through a door, she
does not mind whether it was open or shut; and most
likely, if she finds it open in a warm summer's day, she
will close it; but if she finds it carefully shut on a
freezing day in midwinter, she will leave it wide open.

I need not tell you what are the opposites of
these habits. The careful and tidy girl has an invariable rule, that saves her a deal of trouble: " A PLACE
FOR EVERY THING, AND EVERY THING IN ITS PLACE."
Go into her room at any time, and you will find

every thing in order. She can go in the dark, and lay
her hand on any article she wants; and hence, she never
adds to her mother's anxiety, by taking a light to
her bed-room. She is so much in the habit of putting
things in their proper place, that she never thinks
of leaving them any where else. She never leaves a
thing at random, where she happens to be using it;
but always puts it where it belongs. When she un-
dresses, every article of her clothing is folded, and laid
together in the order that she will want to take it up
in the morning; so that she loses no time in hunting
for it. Her dress is adjusted with neatness and taste,
every article being in the right place, every button,
every hook, every string, every pin, doing its appropriate work, and nothing left loose and dangling, nor
hanging in a one-sided manner. To whatever part of
the house she goes, she leaves it in the order in which
she found it; for it is her invariable rule, when she
uses any thing belonging to another's department, to
replace it exactly as she found it. And when she takes
hold of a cup of water, a lamp, or an article of
crockery, she is careful to get fairly hold, and then to
move moderately, and not with a flirt; and by this
means, she seldom spills any liquid or breaks any
crockery. If she goes to the library, she is careful to
replace every book or paper she takes in her hand,
exactly as she found it. If she takes a book to read,
she carries it with care, firmly grasped in her hand, and
avoids letting it fall, or hitting it against any thing to
bruise the cover. She holds it in such a manner as
not to strain the back nor crumple the leaves; and if
called away from her reading, she puts in a mark, shuts
it up, and lays it in a safe place. She would as soon
think of using a silver spoon as a book, to put under a
window. And when she has finished reading it, she

carefully replaces it in the library, just where she found it. She does not place it wrong end upwards, nor the title towards the back of the shelf; but puts it in the place where it belongs, makes it stand straight, and shoves it back even with its fellows. All her school books are kept in a neat and tidy manner. No blots of ink, nor pencil marks, nor thumb-prints, nor dog's-ears, any where appear. If she passes through a door into or out of a room where other persons are sitting, she leaves it open or shut as she found it; judging that the persons occupying the room, have adjusted its temperature to their own liking. The great difference between her and the careless girl is, that she *has her thoughts about her*, while the other *never thinks*. "*I did'nt think*," is the careless girl's excuse; and that excuse is worse than the careless act itself.

III. There is another very uncomfortable habit, which, for the want of a better name, I shall call NOISINESS. It is made up of talkativeness, loud laughing, humming patches of song-tunes, and in general, a noisy, bustling activity. *Talkativeness* itself is a very bad habit for a little girl or a young lady. It is a good thing to be sociable, and to converse freely and affably at the proper time, and in the proper place. But there is as much difference between this and talkativeness, as there is between the quiet, purling stream, and the noisy, babbling brook. "The tongue of the wise," says Solomon, "useth knowledge aright; but the mouth of fools poureth out foolishness." In the margin it reads, *belcheth* or *bubbleth*. The thoughts of the heart come belching out like water from a bottle, without regard to sense, order, or arrangement, as though the chief object of the tongue were to make a noise. And one that is always babbling must needs talk nonsense, for want of something sensible to say. A talkative girl

will tell all she knows, and all she can remember that
she has ever heard any body say, to every one she
meets. She will take up the time and occupy the
attention of others, in relating long, humdrum stories
about matters and things which nobody cares to hear.
You wait with impatience to hear the end of her story,
that you may have a little quiet; but her tongue never
stops, but, like the clapper of a mill, keeps up its incessant clack. Such a habit is very disagreeable to
others, and makes one appear to great disadvantage.
It leads to the constant violation of the principles of good breeding. No one, especially a young
lady, who understands what belongs to good manners,
will presume on her own importance enough to suppose
that others will be pleased to *hear* her talk and noise
all the time. And no well-bred person will think of
obliging others to listen to her against their will. In
listening to the talkative girl, I have often felt an involuntary apprehension for the *little member*, which is
obliged to perform so much labour. It must be made
of stern stuff, or it would wear out, or, at least, grow
weary. It is a wonder that it does not take fire from
mere friction. It is necessary occasionally, to stop a
mill, to let it cool; but the tongues of some people run
incessantly, and yet seem to suffer no injury.

But *noise* is not always confined to the tongue.
There is a noisy way of doing things, which makes one
think that the girl wants to attract notice. We would
not be so uncharitable; for we always like to think well
of others, and of none more so than a sprightly, active
girl. But the thought comes unbidden, when we see
one moving about the house, with a noisy step and a
wide sweep, making the concussion of the atmosphere
itself announce her approach. And we feel an involuntary sense of incongruity, when we see a noisy, bold

girl; it is so contrary to the model which we have formed in our minds of the female character.

The opposite of this habit is QUIETNESS. The quiet girl moves about the house with a modest air, and a gentle step, as if fearful always of disturbing others. She involuntarily shrinks from the gaze of others; and, therefore, she does as little as possible to attract notice. She has, indeed, a *tongue;* but she values it too highly to keep it constantly running. Her silence does not run into a prudish reserve. She speaks with grace when spoken to, or when her sense of propriety sees a fitting occasion. But she never speaks for the mere sake of talking, nor unless she has something to say. She is especially careful not to incommode others by her talk, nor to presume on entertaining them with mere *tittle-tattle.* She loves to *sing;* but she remembers that humming *shreds and patches* of old tunes and songs incessantly, besides the want of taste, may incommode others; and therefore she waits for proper opportunities, when she may blend her voice in harmony with others, or exercise herself in this sweet art by herself.

There is nothing which sheds such a soft lustre upon the female character in youth, as gentleness of spirit, and a modest, quiet behaviour. These traits of character will always make a favourable impression upon strangers; while it is difficult ever to wear off the unpleasant first impression that is made by a bold, noisy, boisterous girl.

IV. There are several other habits that I shall speak of in connection with other things, and therefore omit them here. I shall only notice one more in this place, and that is RUDENESS. This term does not describe any one particular habit, but a great many little ones. Webster defines it thus : "Rough; of coarse manners; unpolished; clownish; rustic." It is not, therefore, a *habit* merely, but a *series of habits;* and these so numerous, that it can hardly be expected that I should do any more than to give a few specimens, to show what I mean by *rude habits.* These I shall mention at random, as they occur to my mind, without any attempt at order or arrangement; presuming that the minds of my readers will immediately suggest a great many more, of similar character. Rudeness manifests itself both in speech and behaviour. The habit of interlarding conversation with *by-words,* or unmeaning phrases thrown in at random, between the sentences, is exceedingly rude, and especially unbecoming in a young lady. If I could write down some conversations of this kind, just as they are spoken, I think the practice would appear so ridiculous, that you would never indulge it. *By-words,* or *by-phrases,* of whatever kind, add nothing to the force or beauty of conversation; but some that are in common use among low-bred people are objectionable, on the score of vulgarity, approaching to profaneness. Such a habit indicates, indeed, a disposition to be profane, restrained only by fear. The use of low expressions, ungrammatical language, and a sort of *chimney-corner dialect,* is a rude habit, which, if indulged, may cost you great effort to overcome. If you would be a well-bred lady, never indulge any habit of this kind; and be particular in your common conversation, to observe the rules of grammar, and of correct taste, yet without affectation of preciseness. By beginning in this manner, you will form the habit of conversing in an easy, pure, and chaste style, free from all rudeness and vulgarity.

Another rude habit of speech, much practised among the young, is *coarse jesting,* running upon one another, with the use of low witticisms upon each other's peculiarities. I do not know that I am able to describe what I mean, so that you will understand me. I would give you a specimen, if I could do so without being rude myself. It is rude and uncivil to seek, even in pleasantry, to wound the feelings of any.

Rudeness of behaviour is almost indefinable. I shall only be able to mention a few things as specimens, such as tilting one's chair; sitting awkwardly; sitting on two chairs; putting the feet on another's chair; rocking; drumming with the fingers or feet; scratching books, furniture, window-frames, or walls; and a hundred other things that might be named, which indicate not only the want of good breeding, but the want of good taste and a sense of propriety. I have seen a little miss come into the room where I have been visiting, and, throwing herself into the rocking-chair, rock violently back and forth, with as much assurance as if she were amusing herself in a swing. I have seen the same thing in a young woman. But, a little girl, or a young lady, who possessed a nice sense of propriety, would not have presumed, on such an occasion, to seat herself in the rocking-chair at all. I once met a young lady, who was attending a boarding-school, and during a few moments' conversation in the street, she busied herself in deliberately forming prints with her foot in the mud!

These are but a few specimens of *rude habits*. What I wish to impress upon you, by these examples, is, the necessity of avoiding the formation of habits which indicate rudeness and want of cultivation. All the habits which you form in early life should be such as you will wish to carry with you to the grave; for it is exceedingly difficult to break up a bad habit.

Illustrations.

HEEDLESSNESS.

ROSALINDA was pretty, gentle, and amiable. But she had one very bad habit. She was so heedless that she scarcely thought what she said or did. As her father and mother were going out to spend the evening, they charged the children to be good; to amuse themselves, but not to be rude or careless, so as to do any mischief. The children minded what they said. They studied their lessons, made no noise, and did not quarrel. Every thing was in order, and they would have passed the evening very happily, but for Rosalinda's heedlessness. She wanted something that was in the closet in her father's library, and she took a candle to find it. Here she committed two faults. She ought not to have gone to her father's library in his absence. But, if she went, she should not have taken a light to a closet, or among her father's papers. But this was not her only fault. After she had got what she wanted, she heedlessly left the candle burning on her father's table, where there was a large heap of papers.

In about a quarter of an hour, Rosalinda smelt

something burning, and, recollecting that she had left a light burning in the study, immediately ran to get it. She had carelessly set the candle on a bundle of papers. It had fallen over, and set the papers on fire; and, as she opened the door, she found herself completely enveloped in smoke. She was affrighted, and cried out aloud. Her brothers and sisters and the servant ran to the spot; but none of them had the presence of mind to pour some water on the fire, which they might easily have done, and put it out, if they had shut the door, so as not to give it air, till they had brought the water; for as yet there was nothing on fire but the papers and the table. But they were so frightened that they could do nothing but cry out, "The house is on fire! O dear! O dear! What shall we do! What shall we do!" While they were thus lamenting, the fire, having burst into a flame on the opening of the door, had spread to the curtains and the drawers, and soon the whole room was on fire. The neighbours saw it, and ran crying "Fire!" and ringing the bells. The tumult was now dreadful. On all sides, people were crying out, "Fire! fire! water! water!" "Here is the fire," said the neighbours: "we must knock at this house." So they broke open the windows, and began to play the engines upon the fire. After two hours, it was put out; but there remained nothing of the house or its contents but a heap of ruins. The children were all saved; but Rosalinda, in the confusion, was severely hurt. The father and mother now arrived; but what was their consternation to find their house reduced to ashes, and themselves to poverty! However, they were thankful that their children were all alive. All this came, in the first place, by Rosalinda's heedless habits. But after the fire was discovered, the house might have been saved by a little thought. Learn from this story,

1. To avoid heedless, careless habits.

2. Never carry a light about the house. It is dangerous for children to carry a light, especially among papers or clothing.

3. If you open the door of a room, and find that a fire has caught, shut the door instantly, and run for some water. Fire cannot spread rapidly without air; and by shutting the door, you may keep it in check, till it can be put out. A large family were once thrown into consternation, on opening the door of a room where there was a fire, and the flames bursting out. The men were so frightened that they could do nothing. But two of the daughters shut the door, and, seizing each a pail, ran for water, and dashing it into the room, shut the door again and ran for more, till in a few minutes they put the fire out, and saved the house.

BE NEAT.

NEATNESS must be cultivated in early life. It is hard to overcome any disorderly or dirty habit which has become confirmed in childhood and youth. But, if such habits are indulged at this period of life, they will afterwards occasion severe mortification. Fanny Freeman, for some years, dressed in black; and she fell into the dirty habit of wiping the point of her pen on her black dress. This habit became so confirmed that she did not mind when she did it. One afternoon, she dressed herself in white, to go some distance on a visit; but, having first to write a letter, she carelessly wiped her pen as usual on her dress. When the carriage drove to the door, and she was about to set her foot on the step, her attention was called to her dress; and, on looking down, she saw long blots of ink crossing each other in all directions, a perfect fright. She blushed to the very ears for shame and mortification, and was obliged to go back to her room, and put on a black dress.

CARELESSNESS.

"Oh, dear!" said Jane, as she came home from Sabbath School, "I cannot please my teacher at all. I learn my lessons well, but she is never pleased with me."

Jane thought the fields looked so pleasant, she would go across them to school, and enjoy the walk among grass and the flowers; but, in doing so, she tore her tippet, bent her bonnet, slit her frock, and stained the bottom all round with the wet grass and dirt. When she came in, her teacher exclaimed, "O Jane! how untidy you come to school! I am quite ashamed of you." When she took her catechism, it was all over with finger-prints and grease-spots; for she had used it after breakfast, without washing her hands. "Oh! what a careless girl!" said her teacher. "What a dirty book! You have had it but a fortnight, and it is not fit to be touched." Then, when she came to recite her hymns, the book was handed to her teacher all over with dirt. She had dropped it in the road, and another girl had stepped on it. "How did this happen?" inquired her teacher. "Another dirty trick, I fear." Another book was torn, one leaf quite out, and another pinned in, wrong end upwards. When her teacher saw this, she told her she was one of the most careless girls she ever saw. And, when she came to give little books to her scholars, she told Jane it was no use to give one to her; for she was so careless, it would soon be lost or torn to pieces. No wonder her teacher could not be pleased with her. No other good traits will make up for this bad habit. A careless girl will try the patience of her father and mother and teacher, and every one else that she has any thing to do with, and her own too. And it is a habit for which there is no excuse. It is easier to be tidy than careless. "But how is that?" you say. "I find it very difficult to be tidy; and mother chides me every day for my carelessness." I mean, it is easier, all things considered; or, as they say, *"in the long run."* You make yourself a great deal of unnecessary work by your careless habits. I dare say, if you are a careless girl, fourteen years old, you have spent more than a month *hunting for your scissors.* If you doubt this, use a little arithmetic, and see if I am not right. Do you not spend, on an average, a quarter of an hour every day, hunting for your scissors? In six years, that would be twenty-four days. And, suppose you have done the same with respect to three other articles, you have lost an hour a day, just in hunting for your things; and this, in six years, would be four months. All this time might be saved, if you would be careful, when you use any thing, to put it in its place again. But this is not all that is lost by carelessness. You destroy your books, tear your clothes, injure furniture, lose your own patience, and your mother's approbation. When you take all these things into consideration, I think you will agree with me, that it is cheaper and easier to be tidy and careful, than it is to be careless and untidy.

ANOTHER EXAMPLE.

ONE fine spring morning, Laura Selby told her mother that she had mastered her music lesson, and had nothing to do just then; "and now," said she, "pray, be so kind as to lay aside your work, and walk with me."

Just then, their attention was attracted by the sound of the piano. "What is that sound I hear, my love?"

"I dare say it is little George, amusing himself with my piano. I forgot to shut it, when I had finished my lesson."

"I am sorry for that, my daughter, especially as you have so frequently been told to take care of your music. Go, without delay, and close it."

Laura, quite ashamed at her carelessness, as her piano had just been put in tune, ran to obey her mother, and returned, renewing her request for a walk.

Her mother told her that she was going out, and would take her with her, if she could make herself ready without delay. Laura was delighted, and ran quickly to tie on her bonnet and shawl. She was gone longer than seemed necessary. Her mother was obliged to call twice, before she made her appearance, and was about proceeding without her, when she ran hastily through the hall. " My love," said Mrs. Selby, " this is not doing as you ought."

"Mother," said Laura, blushing, "I could not find my shawl for a good while; and then I hunted some time for my pin."

"But where did you put your shawl, that it could not be found?"

"I left it on a chair in the hall, where I sat down a moment, when I came in yesterday, and forgot to put it in my drawer."

"I am grieved, Laura, to find this unfortunate habit of carelessness strengthening, rather than disappearing."

Laura felt ashamed and unhappy. When Mrs. S. had done shopping, they called on Mrs. Ellenwood, and Laura was very happy to find Grace at home; for it was to see her that she had desired to walk. The girls were chatting together in fine spirits, when Mrs. Ellenwood, with a look of pity, inquired what was the matter with Laura's hand, which was wrapt in her handkerchief. "Laura has not injured her hand, I believe," said her mother. "Pray, my dear, why have you twisted your handkerchief over it?"

Laura slowly unrolled her handkerchief, and exhibited a torn glove. "My dear," said her mother, "we must be on our way home; you have employment there, I believe."

Mrs. Ellenwood urged Mrs. S. to let Laura stay and spend the day with Grace, which was what she wanted to do; but her mother would not consent, she was so displeased with Laura's negligence. Laura was sadly mortified; and, when they got into the street, she could not refrain from tears. When they arrived at home, Mrs. S. asked Laura why she went out with her gloves in that condition. "Because," said Laura, "the last time I wore them, I made several holes in them, and —and—I forgot to mend them."

"That is the very thing, my dear, for which you deserve to be reprimanded. Forgetfulness of such duty arises from carelessness. If you exhibit yourself every day, with some part of your dress out of order, your habits of carelessness will be confirmed, and your character, as an untidy young lady, quite established. I am particularly mortified with your appearance to-day, and recommend that you spend the remainder of it in repairing your clothes."

There is, perhaps, no other habit which interferes so much with a girl's happiness, and contributes so much to spoil her temper, as carelessness. A mother does not take delight in chiding her girls, but how can she help it, if they are careless? The snail, as it crawls along on the earth, leaves a track behind it; and so does an untidy girl. Her things are always out of place; and not only her own things, but every thing else that she touches. She forgets to put any thing in its place. Her clothes are disordered; and if there is a rent any where in her wardrobe, she *forgets* to mend it till the moment it is wanted. And these things are so continually occurring, that her mother is obliged to spend half her breath in fruitless efforts to correct this disagreeable habit. Thus, her own temper is fretted and injured, not only by the inconvenience to which she is subjected by her own carelessness, but by the constant displeasure of her mother. This will be tenfold worse if she lives to have a family of her own.

If you would have it sunshine about you, be neat and tidy.

DRINKING WINE.

At a temperance meeting, some years ago, an address was made by Rev. Albert Barnes, in which he showed that alcohol is formed by fermentation; so that it exists in wine, cider, and beer, along with other matter. But, to form ardent spirits, it is separated and thrown off by heat. After the address was finished, a gentleman rose and said he wished to say a word or two to a lady who had refused to sign the pledge; giving as a reason, that she now and then loved to take a little wine. It has been shown, said he, that, when a little wine, or a little beer, or a little cider, is exposed to heat, the alcohol is thrown off. This is called *distillation*. Now, when the lady takes a little wine into the warm stomach, the alcohol is thrown off through " the worm of the still;" up it flies into the brain, and if it does not blow off the cap, it may play mischief there not very creditable. Every time, therefore, that a lady takes a little wine, or a little cider, or a little beer, she is *converted into a distillery!* I think my readers will resolve never to taste a drop of intoxicating liquors, lest they should, unfortunately, be turned into such a loathsome object.

PUTTING PINS IN THE MOUTH.

IT is a very dangerous habit to carry pins in the mouth. A servant girl, in the town of Gore, Upper Canada, some years ago, in taking down some clothes that were pinned on a line, put the pins in her mouth; several of which she accidentally swallowed. One of them stuck in her throat, and the pain, occasioned by the surgeon in removing it, threw her into convulsions. But the pins which she had swallowed occasioned terrible pains in her stomach and bowels and made her very sick, so it was thought she could not live.

DR. JOHNSON'S IDEA OF ELEGANCE IN DRESS.

DR. JOHNSON,[1] speaking of a lady who was celebrated for dressing well, remarked, "The best evidence that I

[1] SAMUEL JOHNSON, LL.D., one of the greatest literary characters of the 18th century, author of a dictionary that has done more, perhaps, than any other to settle the English

can give you of her perfection in this respect is, *that one can never remember what she had on.*" Delicacy of feeling in a lady, will prevent her putting on any thing calculated to attract notice; and yet, a female of good taste will dress so as to have every part of her dress correspond. Thus, while she avoids what is showy and attractive, every thing will be adjusted so as to exhibit symmetry and taste.

FONDNESS FOR DRESS.

EMMA returned from a visit to her uncle's, vexed and unhappy. Her father, perceiving it, invited her to take a walk with him. On their way, they passed the shop of a fashionable dressmaker, when Emma exclaimed, "This is where Aunt purchased Maria's new pelisse, father. You cannot think what a contrast there was in hers and mine. One looked so *nicely,* and the other so *old fashioned and shabby,* I was ashamed to walk with her." "I am very sorry for that," said her father. "Yet if you had not told me, I should not have discovered any thing so mean in your pelisse. However, since wearing it exposes you to so serious a mortification, I will make you a present of a new pelisse like Maria's, if your mother has no objection." Emma thanked him heartily, and her good humour returned.

The object of the walk was to visit a little girl, belonging to the Sabbath School, who had been absent

language. He was a man of taste, a poet, and a moralist. He wrote some of the finest productions which our language affords. He was the son of a bookseller, born at Litchfield, in 1709. He was educated at Oxford, and lived mostly in London. He died, a Christian, in 1784.

several weeks from sickness. They found her pale, emaciated, and dejected, sitting, in a cold day, by a few dying coals in the grate. She was just recovering from a violent fever.

"Where is your mother, my good girl?" inquired Emma's father. The little girl told him that her father's wages were insufficient to support the family, and her mother had lost much time in taking care of her. She was gone out to work, to get something for her and six other little children to eat.

By this time, Emma's face was suffused with tears; and as they went out, she entreated her father to send some coals to keep them warm, and some food for them to eat. But he told her that he could not afford it; for her pelisse would cost as much as they could spare for a long time to come. "Forgive me, my dear father," she said, "and since vanity can only be gratified by such cruel selfishness as this, I hope I shall never again be ashamed, if my clothes are not so expensive or fashionable as Maria's." Nothing is more foolish than to ape others in dress. If you see some that can dress better than yourself, you may easily find others who cannot dress so well. This will cure your vanity.

EYES AND NO EYES.

EVERY thing in nature is beautiful. God delights in beauty; and he has made every thing full of it. But many things are so nicely formed, that one who only looks carelessly around will not see their beauty. The consequence is, some people go moping through life, seldom seeing any thing to admire; while others never behold the face of nature without being enraptured with the beauty of God's works.

A little girl, named Mary, whose parents lived in the city, was spending the summer with her aunt in the country, and going to school with her cousin Helen. One morning, Mary began to wish herself back in the city, and to complain that there was nothing to be seen or heard in the country. Helen felt a little disturbed at this: and the two cousins were on the point of a serious difference, when they were joined by Helen's sister Lucy, five years older than they, who proposed to accompany them to school. The little girls recovered their temper in a moment, subdued by the sweet tones of Lucy's voice, who was a kind-hearted sister, and who took delight in making the younger ones happy. She had overheard their conversation; and her object was to show Mary that the country was full of beauty, if she would but open her eyes to see it.

"Stop a moment," said Helen, as they were in the court-yard, "I must make up a bouquet for the school-mistress."

"And so will I, too," said Mary. So they gathered white and red roses, and pinks, and convolvulus, and Lucy gave them some sprigs from geraniums which were standing in pots, and they each formed a pretty little bouquet. "Do you go directly to school?" inquired Lucy.

"O! no. My aunt sends us off three quarters of an hour before school-time, which she wishes us to spend in the open air; but I am sure ten minutes would be enough; there is nothing to be seen but those dingy old rocks; and I am tired of them."

They were just then going past a little clump of bushes. "What is that fluttering and chirping?" said Lucy.

The children went up on tiptoe, and peered into the bushes. They saw a dear little robin's nest, with three smooth spotted egs, lying in the bottom of it. "O how pretty!" said Helen, "but we won't touch them, will we, Mary? we will just take a peep at them, and then twine the branches together, so that the boys shall not see it; and we will bring some crumbs for the robin every day, and some cherries, won't we, Mary?"

"Yes," said Mary. "I'll leave part of my biscuit now;" and she crumbled a little piece on the grass under the nest. We will call this *our* robin, and this shall be *our* robin's nest; and we won't let any body touch it, nor come near it, till the little birds are out of the shell, and have learned to fly."

Presently they came to a low bridge which crossed a pretty brook. Lucy stepped on the bridge. "Pray, Lucy, what are you looking at?" inquired Mary.

"I am seeing how bright the golden sands look in the bottom of the brook; and how prettily the lights and shadows crinkle through the water. And see what a quantity of pretty flowers grow on its margin. I wish I had some of them." The two little girls ran down the bank, and gathered each a handful of iris and cardinal flowers, and Lucy made a bouquet which they declared to be prettier than those they had brought from the garden. They walked on.

"What a beautiful pile of rocks that is before us," said Lucy. "How prettily the sides are stained with lilac and green and brown, and what a fantastic old pine tree that is on the top. What a nice picture it would make. I wish you would lend me your porcelain slate and pencil for a few minutes, Mary." Mary took them from her straw school-basket, and Lucy sat down upon a bank, and began to sketch the pile of rocks. As she did so, she gave a kind of playful lecture on drawing to the little girls.

"I must begin;" said she, "with a line for the bottom of the rocks, not straight, because they go up and down, here and there.   Now, I observe that the pile of rocks is about half as high as it is broad; and here is a sharp point, and there is a round outline.   Here is a monstrous crevice, and there is a great crack; and here is a queer one-sided stone, with some bushes growing round it; and on the very top is the old pine tree, with its rough trunk and scare crow branches.   Here a line and there a dot; and now for the shading; the straight lines, and the cross lines, and the zigzag lines.   Here it must be left light, for the sun shines brightly upon it; and there it must be dark, for it is in shadow; and those great cracks must be almost black; and I must not forget the little tufts of grass and flowers springing up here and there.   Now, how do you like my picture?"

Helen thought it was pretty, but Mary was in an ecstacy.   It seemed to her like magic.   "O! how I should like to draw from nature; and how pretty these rocks look to me now.   Do let me try to draw them."

Lucy advised her to begin with a single stone, or bush, or flower.   "Try that little crooked tree." Mary looked at it very attentively, and then she tried to draw it.   She got the trunk and branches very well, but when she came to the foliage it looked stiff and unnatural.   "My branches look just like cabbage-heads," said she.   Lucy took her pencil, and showed her on the corner of her slate just the kind of lines she ought to make, and after that, she succeeded admirably. She really made a very pretty little tree.   She could not express her pleasure at her own success.   "Mother always said I had a genius for drawing; and now I intend to draw something every day, and you shall tell me what is wrong." Lucy promised she would; and then they went on.

The school-house stood just the other side of a little wood which they had to pass through. When they had got about half way through the wood, they saw a grey squirrel run up the trunk of a tree, and seat himself on one of the lower branches. "O! what a pretty creature. I wonder if he would run away if we were to go nearer. Let us try." So they stepped carefully over the grass and leaves, until they got near the squirrel, which seemed quite tame, and peered at them very knowingly out of his little grey eyes, as he sat gnawing at an acorn. "Only see his little, sharp teeth!" said Mary, "and how cunning he looks sitting there, with his broad flat tail rising up on his head like a feather. He seems to be a happy little creature. Don't you think he is, Lucy?"

"Yes," said Lucy; "and every nook and corner of the woods and fields is full of innocent little creatures, which a kind Providence has made to live and be happy."

"I never saw them," said Mary; "where are they? I can see nothing now but this squirrel."

"Listen," said Lucy. "Do you hear nothing?"

"I hear some birds singing. Oh! I forgot the birds. Yes, there are plenty of them, and happy enough they are."

"Can you hear nothing else?"

"Nothing but a confused sound, as if a thousand crickets and catydids and grasshoppers were singing together."

"Which in truth they are. They are on every side of you, and under your feet, singing away as merrily as can be. But do you hear nothing else?"

"I hear the bleating of lambs," said Helen, and the peeping of frogs, from yonder brook. Let us go to the brook." They did so; and looking attentively into the deepest places, they saw that it was filled with pretty little fishes, darting and playing about.

"Oh! how pretty,' said Mary; and how happy they seem to be too, although they do not make a noise. But what is that? Is it possible that it is the school-bell? We must run. Good bye, dear Lucy, kind Lucy, sweet Lucy; good bye."

The next morning the girls did not wait to be urged off to school, they were ready ten minutes before the time; for, as Mary said, she longed to see if the little robin's nest was safe; and she wished very much to try a little corner of the clump of rocks; and to gather some cardinal flowers and iris. "And then, you know, Helen, we are to look for the squirrel, and carry him some nuts. And I want to find a catydid, which my aunt says is such a curious creature. And I wish to take another peep at the fishes, to see if there are any like those in the book that Lucy showed us last evening. I really do not think we shall ever find the walk to school dull again." The reason of this change was, that Mary had just *opened her eyes,* while before she *kept them shut.*

CHAPTER XII.

THE reader will perhaps laugh at the idea of *educating* the body. But a moment's reflection will show that no part of man more needs education than the body. The design of education, as I have already said, is, to form the character, and prepare us, in early life, for what we are to do in future. For this purpose, the body needs discipline as well as the mind. An ill body makes an ill mind and a sad heart. The health of the body is necessary to the healthy operation of the mind; and a healthy body is secured by activity. But the body not only needs *health,* but discipline. The fingers must be taught all manner of handiwork, and exercised upon it, in order to accustom them to the use that is to be made of them; the feet must be taught to perform their appropriate duties, in a graceful and proper manner; and all the muscles of the body must be exercised, in due proportion, to give them strength and solidity. The proper discipline of the several members of the body is necessary, not only to prepare them for useful occupation, but to give them a graceful, natural, and easy motion, and so promote good manners and a genteel carriage.

I shall not be very particular in what I have to say on this subject, but only give a few gentle hints.

1. DISCIPLINE THE BODY TO OBEY THE WILL. You would not think, to see some young folks, that the will had any thing to do with the movements of the body; for it moves in all imaginable ways, with all sorts of contortions. First flies out a foot, then a hand, then there's a twirl or a swing, then a drumming of the fingers, a trotting of the foot, or some such odd figure. This arises from leaving the body to control itself, by its own natural activity, the mind taking no super-vision of its motions. Now, if you early accustom yourself to exercise a strict mental supervision over the body, so as never to make any movement what-ever, except what you mean to make, you will find this habit of great consequence to you; for, besides sav-ing you the mortification of a thousand ungraceful movements which habit has rendered natural, it will enable you to *control your nerves,* the necessity for which you will understand better hereafter than you do now. Make the *will* the ruling power of your body, so as never to do any thing but what you mean to do, and you will never get the reputation of *being nervous.*

2. AVOID LATE HOURS. It would seem hardly necessary to give such a direction to young persons still under the control of their parents. But facts too plainly show that parents do not always sufficiently consider the injurious effects of late hours upon the fair and healthy development of the human frame. And the disposition of young people to seek amusement, overcomes, with them, the dictates of prudence. But the practice of sitting up late, and especially of being abroad late at night, is a war upon nature. It inter-rupts the regular course of things. It turns night into day and day into night. If you would be pale-faced, sickly, nervous, and good for nothing, sit up late at night.

3. RISE EARLY. It is said that, to have a fair skin, rosy cheeks, and a fine complexion, one must wash every morning in summer *in the dew*. Whether there is any virtue in the dew or not, I cannot say; but I have no doubt that such would be the effect of the practice proposed. To rise early, before the atmosphere has become heated with the summer's sun, and walk abroad, snuffing the cool breeze, listening to the music of the feathered tribe, and joining in the sweet harmony of nature, hymning forth praise to the Creator, certainly tends to promote health of body and cheerfulness and serenity of mind; and these will make a blooming countenance, and clothe very plain features with an aspect of beauty. The adding of the *dew wash* will do no harm. If you make a rule of washing in the dew, it will stimulate you to sally forth before the sun has driven it away; and you can find no softer water than the dew.

4. USE PLENTY OF WATER. The body cannot be kept in a healthy state, without frequent bathing. It should be washed all over, with cold water, at least once every day, to promote health and cleanliness. One who has never tried it can have no idea of its invigorating effects; and it seems hardly possible that the human system can keep long in order, while this is neglected. The machinery of a watch, after a while, gets dirty, so that it will not run till it is taken to pieces and cleaned. But the machinery of the human body is vastly more intricate than that of a watch. It is made up of an endless number of parts, of various patterns, some of them of the most delicate texture and exquisite workmanship, but all parts of a great machine that is constantly in motion. And there is provision made for carrying off all the dirt that accumulates on its wheels and bands, in little tubes, which discharge it upon the surface of the skin. But unless frequently washed

I

off, it accumulates, and stops up the ends of these little tubes, and prevents their discharging, so that the offensive and poisonous matter which they would carry off is kept in the system. Let this go on a little while, and it cannot fail to produce disease. Therefore, I say, *use plenty of water.*

5. TAKE CARE OF YOUR TEETH. The teeth have a very important office to perform in the animal economy; that of preparing the food for the stomach. What is not done by the teeth must be done by the digestive organs. Therefore, your health is deeply concerned in the preservation of a good set of teeth. The voice and the countenance, also, plead with you to take care of your teeth. In almost all cases, teeth may be saved from decay, if attended to in time. The best directions I can give for preserving the teeth are, to clean them every day with a brush, and pick them after every meal with a pointed quill, so as to remove all the particles of food from between them, and the tartar that adheres to the surface; cleanliness, as well as the safety of the teeth, requires this. You ought to have your teeth examined and attended to, by a dentist, once or twice a year. Keeping them clean preserves them from decay; and if decay commences, a dentist can stop it, if he can take them in season.

6. BE ACTIVE. The body was made *for use.* Every part of it is formed for activity. But any thing made for use will suffer injury to lie still. The human body, especially, if suffered to remain inactive, becomes useless. Activity strengthens the parts. If you would have more strength, you must use what you have, and it will increase. The right use of your members, also, must be learned by *practice.* Much practice is necessary, for instance, to train the fingers to the various uses in which they are to be employed, so as, (to use a

homely phrase,) to make them *handy*. The body, like-wise, needs exercise, to keep it in a healthy state. The various parts of its machinery have a great work to do, every day, in turning your food into blood, and sending it a great many thousand times, in a vast number of little streams, to every part of the body. But this machinery will not work, if the body is all the time in-active. It requires *motion*, to give it power. There is nothing, therefore, so bad for it as *laziness*. It is like a dead calm to a windmill, which stops all its machinery.

7. LEARN, AT PROPER TIMES, TO BE STILL. All nature needs repose. If the human system were always kept in the utmost activity, it would soon wear out. For this reason, God has given us periodical seasons of rest: a part of every day, and one whole day in seven. There are times, also, when it is not proper to be active; as, when you are at your devotions, or at family worship, or in the house of God. So, likewise, at school, or in company, or when you sit down with the family at home, as well as in many other cases, activity is out of place. Your body, therefore, will never be *educated*, till you have obtained such control over it, as to be able, at proper times, to *be still.* And I may say, it is a great accomplishment in a young person, to know just when to be still, and to have self-control enough to be still just at the proper time.

8. BE CAREFUL TO KEEP THE BODY IN ITS NATURAL POSITION. This is necessary, not only to preserve its beauty, but to prevent deformity. Sitting at school, or at any sedentary employment, is liable to produce some unnatural twist or bend of the body. The human form, in its natural position, is a model of beauty. But, when bad habits turn it out of shape, it offends the eye. Avoid a stooping posture, or an inclination

to either side.   But sit and stand erect, with the small of the back curved in, the chest thrown forward, the shoulders back, and the head upright.   A little attention to these things every day, while the body is growing, aud the bones and muscles are in a flexible state, will give your form a beauty and symmetry, which you can never acquire afterwards, if you neglect it at this time of life.   And it will do more, a thousand times, to keep you in health, than all the doctor's pill-boxes.

9. AVOID TIGHT-DRESSING AS YOU WOULD A BLACK SNAKE.   You will perhaps smile at this.   But if you know any thing of the black snake, you will recollect that it assaults not with deadly venom, but winds itself around its victim, stops the circulation of the blood, and, if it reaches high enough, makes a rope of itself, to strangle him.   I need not tell you that the effects of tight-dressing are similar.   Whatever part of the body, whether neck, chest, arms, limbs, or feet, is *pinched* with tight covering, is subject to the same strangling process produced by the black snake.   It obstructs the free circulation of the blood, and produces a tendency to disease in the part so compressed.   If you feel an unpleasant tightness in any part of your dress, *remember the black snake.*

10. DISCIPLINE THE MUSCLES OF THE FACE.   You may think this is a queer direction; but I assure you it is given with all gravity.   If you allow every temper of the heart to find a corresponding expression in the muscles of the face, you will be sure to spoil the fairest countenance.   How would you feel, if you were to see an accomplished young person, with fine features, and a beautiful countenance; but on coming near, should discover little holes in the face, from which, every now and then, vipers and venomous serpents were thrusting out their heads and hissing at you?

Well, the evil tempers of the heart, such as pride, vanity, envy, and jealousy, are a nest of vipers; and, when indulged, they will spit out their venom through the countenance. How often do we see a proud, scornful, sour, morose, or jealous expression, that has fairly been worn into the features of the countenance! And what is this but the hissing of vipers that dwell within? Strive to acquire such self-control, as to keep a calm, serene expression upon your countenance; and you cannot tell how much it will add to your appearance.

11. BE TEMPERATE. To be strictly temperate is, to *avoid all excess*. Not only abstain from eating and drinking what is hurtful, but use moderation in all things; in eating and drinking, in running and walking, in play, in amusement.

CHAPTER XIII.

KNOWLEDGE OF HOUSEHOLD AFFAIRS.

IT is in acquiring a knowledge of household affairs, chiefly, that your body is to be educated. Young girls often have wrong notions about this matter, looking upon *house-work* as mere drudgery, only fit for servants. And, especially, if they get it into their heads that they are to be trained up for ladies, they learn to despise all useful labour. And sometimes they become so heartless and unfeeling as to be willing to see their mothers working like slaves, while they set up for ladies. But this is any thing but lady-like. The term *lady* was originally applied to a woman of rank, as that of *lord* was to a man of rank. In the old country, society is divided into different orders, the *nobility* and the *common people*. But it is not so among us. Every woman can be a lady, who conducts herself in a lady-like manner. And the true idea of a lady is, a strict propriety of conduct on all occasions. One may, therefore, be a lady as well in the kitchen as in the parlour.

Nothing will make a woman appear more ridiculous than a contempt for useful occupation, and especially for household affairs. No woman that has the charge of a family can carry out the true idea of a lady, without a knowledge of household duties. She cannot have things done to her mind, nor save herself from the severest mortification, without it.

Some would-be ladies affect great contempt for labour, and especially scorn to put their hands to any household work. They are afraid of soiling their hands, or of having it known among their fashionable friends that they are in the habit of doing any thing *useful*. But such ladies are always unhappy; because they are obliged to be dependent on servants, and they can never get those who will do work to suit them, unless they know how to do it themselves, and are able to give instruction to those whom they employ. They are, likewise, despised by all sensible people; for the greatest merit any one can have, in the estimation of the people of this country, is, *to be useful*. But a lady who does not know how to take care of herself and of her own house, or who feels above it, cannot be very useful. She will, most likely, be a *laughing-stock* among the people. The greater portion of the women of this country, with the assistance of their daughters, do their own work; and some of the most accomplished ladies I have ever seen are not ashamed, when there is occasion for it, to go into the kitchen and cook a meal of victuals. And why should they be? Christian ladies are called by the apostle Peter the daughters of Sarah; and she cooked a supper with her own hands for the angels that came to visit Abraham. King Solomon represents his virtuous woman as seeking wool and flax, and working willingly with her hands, and as rising early and giving meat to her household. No one need be ashamed to be seen engaged in any useful employment; but it is a great shame for any woman who has charge of a house, not to understand how to do what is necessary to manage a house. There is much to interest the mind in household affairs. You may apply your philosophy to sweeping and dusting, and making beds, and find interesting illustrations of what you learn from books in all the arrangements of the house; and in cooking and washing you will find abundance of interesting experiments in chemistry. Yet there are multitudes who would prefer spending their time at fancy needle-work, though there is very little required in performing it but mechanical skill. This I do not condemn; but the useful should be set foremost. All ornamental branches of education are to be encouraged; but they will not make amends for the want of skill to cook a meal of victuals, make a plain garment, or darn a stocking. There is more science in boiling a potato, or raising bread, and more judgment required, than there is in executing the finest piece of embroidery. Should you ever become the mistress of a house, your ornamental work will please the sight; but it will never set off against heavy bread, and hard watery potatoes.

Illustrations.

MRS. BRADISH.

"It is the middle of January. Business is brisk, and winter parties are frequent. At half-past eight o'clock in the morning, a girl stands at the foot of Mrs. Bradish's broad stairs, ringing the bell for breakfast. She returns into the back parlour, and after walking and fidgeting about for a while, begins talking to herself: 'I wish Mrs. Bradish would ever come to her meals when the bell rings. She stays half an hour, and then scolds because every thing is cold. I'm sure it isn't my fault; there was full an hour and a quarter between the two bells this morning; but she's just as likely to be in time when I allow only fifteen minutes. I'm determined I won't get up so early another morning, that's poz—' She was interrupted by Mr. Bradish's appearance, in morning gown and slippers.

"'Why, Bridget, why did you not ring a first bell? Here it is half-past eight o'clock; just the hour I promised to meet a western merchant at my store. I shall lose a thousand dollars.'

"'I did ring a first bell, sir.'

"'Not at the regular hour.'

"'We can't have no regular hours, sir. Sometimes the cook isn't up till eight o'clock, and we can't have no fire in the kitchen. And sometimes Mrs. Bradish isn't ready for her breakfast till nine o'clock; and she doesn't like it, if it's cold.'

"'But I must have my breakfast at eight o'clock. Come, hurry! give me a cup of coffee. This egg is as hard as a stone, and as cold as an icicle. Bring me some hot cakes.'

"The cakes were brought. 'These cakes are sour; they are not fit to be eaten. What is the reason we always have sour cakes?'

"'I don't know. The last cook used to put in some white stuff to sweeten them, but I don't think this one knows. She don't seem to know much about cooking.'

"'It must be soda, or pearlash. Go to her, and tell her to put some into her batter. Run up first, and ask Mrs. Bradish to come down to her breakfast.'

"Mrs. Bradish and the remodelled cakes made their appearance at about the same time. The former looked dull, listless, and sleepy, with a stray lock of uncombed hair hanging down from beneath a tumbled cap. The latter, that is, the cakes, were of a dark sea-green colour, and sent forth an odour very much resembling that from a soap-boiler's vat. Mr. Bradish swallowed one mouthful; but, on taking a second, he was obliged to walk hastily to the window, where he threw something into the back yard. He returned to the table, making very wry faces.

"'Bridget, bring me a cracker, if there is one in the house. My dear, don't eat that bread or those cakes; you will be poisoned. I took a whole mouthful of pure saleratus just now. How I wish we could ever have a pleasant breakfast together, with things hot, and nice, and well-cooked!'

" 'I'm sure it is not my fault; I tell the cook to make them nice.'

" 'Suppose, my dear, you were, for one or two mornings, to get up early, and go into the kitchen to see that things were properly prepared.'

" 'How can I get up early, when I am out, almost every night, till one or two o'clock?'

" 'Let us go to fewer parties, my dear, and not stay so late when we do go. I should be much happier, and my business would be much better attended to. I think our servants need overseeing.'

" 'Very well, Mr. Bradish. If you wish me to spend my time cooking, and overseeing servants, you should have told me so at first, that I might have learned how. My hands will look pretty in the evening, with the nails all filled with pie-crust. And how can I dance the Polka with any spirit, if I'm to be dancing from the kitchen to the parlour all day?'

"Just at that moment, there was a heavy thump and a loud squall overhead. 'There, that careless little Jane has dropped the baby on the floor. I hope she has not broken any of its bones.'

"Charles Bradish really loved his wife and child. He followed her up stairs, but seeing the baby was not seriously hurt, he kissed them both, and hurried away. Just as he left the room, he said, 'My old friend, Horatio Snelling, is in town. If I see him to-day, I must ask him home to dinner; and, pray, my dear, be punctual, and have things nice and well served. He is one of my best customers, and he has a capital wife at home.'

" 'I do wonder,' said Mrs. Bradish, 'what Charles must be bringing people home to dinner for. It is a perfect bore. And how in the world a nice dinner is to be got with a cook just out of an Irish bog, is more than I can tell. It is really a reasonable, pretty thing, to expect me to spend half of my time in the kitchen, teaching and coaxing those that ought to know their business before they come to me!'

At eleven o'clock, however, she went into the kitchen. The marketing had just come: a turkey, a leg of mutton, and a fine fresh fish. 'Well, Biddy, I suppose you know how to cook these things. The turkey must be roasted, with a brown gravy made of the giblets. The leg of mutton boiled with caper-sauce; the fish must also be boiled and garnished with eggs. Make an apple pie, and some custards; that will be quite sufficient for a second course. And be sure, Biddy, to have it all hot and ready for the table at exactly half past three o'clock.'

"Biddy said she knew perfectly well how it should be done, and that it should all be ready at the moment.

"Mrs. Bradish dressed, and went out to order a new head-dress for the evening party. She met a friend who wished her to go shopping; and time slipped away so fast in this manner, that it was three o'clock when she came in. She ran to the kitchen to see what state the dinner was in. The turkey was browning very nicely before a hot fire; and the cook assured her that the mutton and the fish were doing very well. The pies were yet in the oven, but the custards were of such a dingy colour, and so burnt upon the outside of the cups, that Susan saw they would not answer to be placed upon the table. 'I can make a tipsy-cake; Charles likes it, and it will look very well.' She sent the girl to the nearest confectioner's for a sponge cake, while she beat up cream, sugar, and spices. The cake was brought.

"'Now run up stairs, and bring down a bottle of wine or brandy, from the dining-room closet.'

"The bottle was brought, and part of the contents poured into a dish. The cake was then laid carefully in, and the custard poured around it. 'There, that looks nicely; and how quickly it was done! I did it all myself too.' Saying which, she ran up stairs to change her dress for dinner.

"She did not get down in time to receive her husband's friend; but just as she reached the parlour door, the bell rang for dinner, so they passed at once to the dining-room. The meats were all on the table; but it looked bare, for a dish of potatoes, boiled with the skins on, was the only vegetable. The waiter-girl was sent in haste for some currant jelly, and the fish was uncovered. It was in pieces or flakes, and of a pale brown colour. It was garnished with eggs, one of which was streaked with green, and which sent forth such a peculiar odour, that the dish had to be sent at once from the table. 'This turkey looks well,' said Mr. Bradish; 'but I fear it is not done,' continued he, as the passage of the knife disclosed the raw, pink-coloured meat. No, the turkey had been too suddenly cooked; there was not a bit even of the bread that was eatable. Susan looked in despair; but her husband, seeing her mortification, tried to put a good face upon the matter. 'Well, we must dine upon mutton; and there have been worse things eaten than a good leg of boiled mutton.'

"Mr. Snelling declared it was his favourite dish.

"'But how is this?' exclaimed Mr. Bradish, at the first mouthful; 'it tastes of fish more than mutton. It must have been boiled with the fish.'

"There are certain flavours whose union is pleasant; but mutton and fish do not happen to be of that kind. Mr. Snelling, however, was good-natured and polite. He peeled a potato, helped himself to currant jelly, and appeared to eat with infinite relish, telling all the laughable anecdotes he could think of, about the bulls and mistakes of both foreigners and natives. Neither Charles nor his wife, however, could converse with any spirit; and they both looked relieved, when the dishes were taken away. Susan hoped that the apple pie would prove eatable; but she was mistaken: the crust was hard and leathery, and the apples half-baked and ill-flavoured. The custard cake was her last and only hope. 'Let me help you to some of this, Mr. Snelling,' said she, filling a plate full. 'I flatter myself you will find it good, for I made it myself. Our dinner has proved so very poor, I hope you will eat heartily of it.'

"Charles brightened up. He looked at his friend, hoping to hear him praise his wife's cookery. His guest had a spoonful of the liquid cake in his mouth. His face flushed, his teeth were set together, while a peculiar heaving motion of the chest showed any thing but a gratified palate. At last, with a tremendous effort, he swallowed it.

"'What is it?' said Charles, looking aghast, and at the same time tasting the dish before him. 'Oh! it is saturated with nauseous drugs! This is not wine; it is elixir pro!' It was true; the girl in her hurry, had mistaken the bottle.

"The friend was a humourist, and the whole affair of the dinner, Mrs. Bradish's chopfallen countenance, and her husband's rueful looks, struck him all at once so ludicrously, that he could not refrain from laughing long and heartily. Few people could resist that laugh, and Charles was finally obliged to join; but his wife had been too much mortified, and was now too angry, to partake in their merriment; so she betook herself to her nursery."

If Mrs. Bradish had been in the habit of working

in the kitchen, when she was a girl, and if her mother had made it an important part of her education to learn household affairs, she would never have suffered these mortifications.

LEARNING TO WORK.

POOR and helpless will that woman be, who does not learn, when a girl, to employ her hands in useful labour. She may have enough, but she will not know how to use it for the comfort of her family. She may be well educated, and able to converse interestingly. She may play well on the piano. And all this is well. But, if she does not understand *work*, her common, every-day duties cannot be well done; and these are what, in all circumstances, contribute most to the comfort of every-day life.

NEW MUSIC.

AN accomplished young lady stepped to the door, on the ringing of the bell, and was greeted by a young gentleman who had called to see her. On entering the parlour, he glanced at the harp and piano, and said, "I thought I heard music: on which instrument were you performing?" "On the *gridiron*," she replied, "with the accompaniment of the *frying-pan*. My mother is without help, and she says that I must learn to finger these instruments sooner or later."

Another young lady, the daughter of a New England clergyman, was visiting a rich uncle, in a great city in a neighbouring State; and, being asked what instrument she played upon, replied, "When I am at home,

I play on the *cooking stove*." These young ladies had the good sense not to be ashamed of useful labour. It is a fine thing to know how to finger the piano, and play on the harp; but these accomplishments are a poor substitute for the ability to play on the cooking stove.

MAKING BREAD.

Good bread is one of the necessaries of life. With it, one can make a meal, though every thing else on the table be inferior. Without it, no one can make a comfortable meal. But to make good bread is a very great art, and one that every girl ought to learn in her mother's house.

There was a young lady, who had been brought up in fashionable style, and was really quite accomplished; but, her parents being wealthy, she was under no necessity of labouring, and she was educated without any practical knowledge of household affairs. She was married; and for some time things went on very well, for she happened to have an excellent cook. But, after a while, her cook left her; and, as good help was scarce, she took such a girl as she could get. The first thing Nancy was required to do was to make some bread. But she said she never had done such work before; but, if Mrs. —— would tell her *how*, she could soon learn. And now the lady's eyes were open, the first time, to her mistake. She did not know how herself, and how could she teach Nancy? After considering a moment, she replied, "Upon the whole, as there is so much more that is important to be done, we will put this matter off, and try baker's bread."

After some days, as they were sitting at the table,

the husband inquired, "Cannot Nancy make bread? I am quite tired of baker's bread." "She shall make some," replied the wife; "but this is nice baker's bread; I don't know but it is better than any home-made bread I ever ate." "There is nothing," rejoined he, "like good home-made bread, *such as my mother used to make.*"

Nothing could be more mortifying to a young wife, than to find herself in such a situation. She was quite at a loss what to do. At first, she thought of confessing her ignorance; but as they had now been married some time, she thought it would not do. The bread must be made; but *how?* that was the question. She concluded to begin with pearlash bread, because she thought it would be more easily managed than yeast; but she knew nothing about it, except that it must be made of flour, milk, salt, and pearlash. She concluded she would put in pearlash enough, so as to be sure and have it light. The preparation was made, and it was put in the oven. Mrs. —— sat beside the stove, anxiously awaiting its progress, to see it rise. It grew beautifully brown; but, instead of rising up round and plump, it remained, *flat, flat, flat!* Dinner came. Mr. —— walked in, with a friend or two to dine. They sat down to the table. The mackerel was well broiled; the potatoes were well done; every thing was well, but the bread, the article that her husband considered most important—he took a slice; it did not look like bread, it was thickly studded with little brown spots of undissolved pearlash; and then, how it tasted! a strange mixture of salt and bitter. He looked surprised and mortified. As soon as they were alone, he said, "Had you not better attend to the bread-making yourself, and not leave that most important part of cooking to such miserable, inexperienced hands?" She went away and wept, with this pitiful lamentation,

3   K

"What *shall* I do?" There stood the piano; and there was the handsome worsted work, over which she had spent so many days in her father's house. But of what use were all these fine things *without bread?* She had just discovered that she could not be a good wife, and make her husband and family happy, without knowing how to make bread; and this most important branch of education had been entirely neglected. She was indeed in a dilemma. She, however, had good sense and resolution enough to surmount the difficulty. She resolved, from that moment, to study her domestic duties, and to *know how* to become a skilful, economical, thrifty housekeeper. But she had a long and wearisome trial, before she was able to set before her husband her sweet, light, and wholesome loaves. When she found herself in the sad dilemma that has been described, she would have given all her knowledge of music and embroidery to know how to make good bread. Yet do not understand me as speaking lightly of those accomplishments. They are good in their place, and a great addition to a young lady's education; but they cannot make up for the want of a knowledge of household affairs. And, if my gentle readers will listen to me, I would have them know that there is nothing to be done in managing the house but what they ought to understand how to do, by having done it themselves, and done it repeatedly, till they can do it well. In no other way will they be able to avoid such a disagreeable dilemma as that in which this lady found herself.

HIGH NOTIONS.

A YOUNG gentleman became very much interested in the daughter of a wealthy farmer, and thought of marrying her; but, after a while, he discovered that she was wholly ignorant of domestic affairs. He therefore sought an opportunity to introduce the subject of domestic economy, when she declared her opinion that it was grossly indelicate for a lady of fashionable education to be engaged in domestic concerns. Just then, her mother came in, with her arms full of wood for the fire. Her reflections just before, taken with this fact, would seem to imply that she regarded her mother as a vulgar sort of a woman. At any rate, it showed that she was unfeeling enough to set up for a fine lady, and let her mother do the drudgery of the house. The young man was so disgusted that he never visited her again. Some time afterwards she married a young merchant, who was doing a fair business, and carried her high notions into full operation. With extravagant furniture, numerous servants, and attendant expenses, her husband's affairs became embarrassed, and every thing was seized by his creditors. Poor Zelia had the mortification to return to her father's house, a victim to her conceits: a useless and unhappy creature.

CHAPTER XIV.

By the *heart*, I mean the *moral faculties*, in distinc tion from the *intellectual*. Any action is *moral*, which can be *praised* or *blamed*. The *moral faculties* are those which determine moral action. These faculties are, the *Conscience*, *Will*, and *Affections*. In this division, I do not attempt metaphysical exactness, but only what I can make my readers understand. When I speak of *educating* these faculties, I do not mean to separate the process from that of religious education in general; for nothing can be well done, in the formation of character, without religious principle and motives at the foundation. But my object is, to speak of the specific means by which these faculties may be cultivated.

It may be necessary for me to explain what I mean by the *Conscience, Will*, and *Affections*. Yet it does not fall in with my design, neither would it suit the age and capacities of those for whom I write, to enter into a philosophical description, or analysis, of the faculties of the mind, or affections of the heart. I shall only give such simple explanations as are sufficient for my purpose, and as I suppose will be understood by my readers.

I THE CONSCIENCE. This is the faculty which

determines whether any action proposed to the mind, or any feeling of the heart, is *right* or *wrong*. If you will watch the motions of your own mind, you will perceive, whenever any thing is proposed to be done or not to be done, something within tells you that it is either *right* or *wrong;* if *wrong,* you find the same *something within,* urging you *not to do* it; or, if *right,* the same impulse moves you *to do* it. If you do as you are thus urged, you find the same voice within *approving* what you have done, or, if you do not obey, *condemning* you. This *something within* is CONSCIENCE.

You have, doubtless, lived long enough to experience many a conflict, or dispute, between your *conscience* and your *inclinations.* You are inclined to do something which your conscience tells you is wrong, but conscience not only tells you it is wrong, but urges you not to do it. Your inclinations, or desires, urge you in the contrary direction; and this creates a conflict. If conscience prevails, then it approves your decision, and you feel happy. But, if inclination prevails, conscience upbraids, and you feel miserable.

As I have defined education, you will see the great importance of *educating the conscience.* It is the leading moral faculty, and must have a great influence upon the moral character. For the conscience itself may be wrong. It is not itself the rule by which you are to determine what is right and wrong. The word of God is the rule. The office of conscience is, to determine whether any thing you propose to do is agreeable to the rule, and to urge you, accordingly, to do it or not to do it. Suppose you wish to determine whether any thing is straight; you lay a rule upon it that you suppose to be straight, and if they agree, that settles the matter. Your eye, comparing the object with the rule, determines whether it is straight or not. But, if the rule applied is crooked, your eye is deceived, and you misjudge. Conscience is the eye of the soul, that compares an action with the rule. The conscience, then, must be well instructed. You must learn the *rule of right* from the Word of God, and then conscience will always decide right. But, if you adopt false notions of right and wrong, your very conscience will lead you astray. The first thing, then, in the education of the heart is, to have it filled with *right principles;* and these you are to obtain from the study of the Bible, and from listening to the instructions of your parents, teachers, and ministers.

The next thing is, *always to obey the voice of conscience.* If you go contrary to it, and do what conscience tells you is wrong, or neglect what it urges upon you as duty, you weaken that faculty, and harden the heart. When you refuse to hearken to the voice of conscience, the next time it will not speak so loud; and every time this is repeated, the weaker it grows, till at length it is scarcely heard at all, and you may go on and sin almost without restraint. If you will look back a little while in your own experience, you will see the force of what I say. If you have ever fallen into the habit of secretly disobeying your parents, you will find an illustration of it. The first time you were tempted to disobey, your conscience was very loud against it; but the temptation, falling in with your inclinations, prevailed. Then conscience upbraided you with a voice of terror. But you were not discovered, and no immediate evil followed. The next time the temptation presented itself, the remonstrance of conscience was feeble, and its condemnation light. The next time it was feebler still; till at length you could do with careless indifference what at first made you shudder. But when the power of conscience is gone, there is but one step more to ruin. If, then, you would keep your conscience tender, you must always obey its voice.

Another means of educating the conscience is, the habit of thinking with approbation of what is right, and putting out of the mind with horror all thoughts of what is wrong. The most hateful things, by becoming familiar to the sight, lose much of the horror which they excite at first. A person who had never seen an animal killed would be deeply affected at the sight; but a butcher thinks nothing of it. So, by thinking much of what is wrong, the conscience becomes defiled, and ceases to act with promptness and decision; while, if kept familiar only with the good, it would revolt instantly from the bad.

II. THE WILL. This is the faculty that *chooses* or *refuses*. It is the *decisive* faculty. It is the power that determines action, whether good or bad. It is the *ruling* faculty of the soul. I said *conscience* was the *leading* faculty, because it goes before the action of the will, and moves it to choose what is right. The *will* is the *ruling* faculty, because it determines all action. The way to *educate the will* is, to accustom it to submit to the dictates of conscience. The will, in our fallen and depraved state, is turbulent and unsubmissive. It is not disposed to submit to the law of God, nor to those whom God has set over us. Yet there is nothing of more importance to our happiness and usefulness than the early subjection of the will. If you determine that you will always have your own will, you will certainly be unhappy; for it is impossible that you should always have your own way. But if you early accustom yourself to give up your own will; to submit to the will of God, as made known to you in his word and Providence; to submit to your parents, as those whom God has set

over you; and to your own conscience, as the faithful
monitor which God has placed in your own bosom: then
you will be as happy as you can be in this imperfect
state.   This you will not accomplish all at once.   It
must be the result of experience, trial, and discipline,
with the grace of God in your heart.   But if you begin
to cultivate the *habit of submission*, in early life, it will
save you many a severe struggle and much unhappiness.
You have doubtless learned, before this time, that you
always get into difficulty at home, when you set out to
have your own will.   And perhaps you have sometimes,
in your impatience at contradiction, secretly wished that
you were of age, beyond the control of your parents,
that you might do as you pleased.   But I assure you,
both from my own experience and from what I have
seen of the world, that you will not find it any easier
to have your own will, after you come to act for yourself.   You will not succeed in any thing you undertake
to do for others, unless you give up your own will;
neither will you succeed in making society agreeable to
yourself.   Suppose you go to a shoemaker, to get a pair
of shoes made, and as soon as you begin to tell him
how you wish them done, he answers, "I understand
my business, if you want a pair of shoes, I'll make them
for you, but nobody can teach me how to do my work?"
You would say, "He is a surly creature; I'll have nothing to do with him."   Or, suppose you go into company, and you find a young lady who will consent to
nothing except what she herself proposes: you say,
"She is a selfish creature; let her enjoy herself alone."
But all this comes from mere wilfulness.   You never
will be comfortable, much less happy, till you are willing
to yield to others, when no principle is concerned, but
only the mere gratification of your own will.   And when
one is employed by another, it is perfectly reasonable

that he should be directed by his employer, even if what he is directed to do may appear to him unwise. The only way that you can succeed, and be happy, in any thing you may undertake to do for others, is, to submit your will to theirs, and do cheerfully, and without objection, what they require: provided, only, that they do not require you to do wrong. If you will look back, you will find that this *wilfulness* has been the cause of all the trouble you have got into with your parents, and of nearly all the altercations you have had with your brothers, sisters, and companions. And, if you retain this disposition, it will make you miserable, whatever station in society you may occupy.

A little boy, named Truman, lost his own mother; and when he was four or five years of age, his father married again. His new mother was an excellent lady, very affectionate and kind-hearted toward the children. But one day, when she was teaching Truman how to read, she could not make him say his lesson correctly. She therefore used the rod till he submitted, and read as he ought. He was afterwards overheard talking with himself, about his conduct: "Tru, what made you treat your dear mother so? Hasn't she always been kind to you?" "Yes, I know she has. She loves me, and tries to do me all the good she can." "Then how could you be so naughty, to treat her so?" "I know I have been a very naughty boy, and treated her very bad indeed when she has been very kind to me; and she was trying then to teach me for my own good." "What can you say for yourself, then? How did you come to behave so?" "I can't say any thing for myself; I know it was very mean. I feel ashamed to think I could treat her so; and I'll never do it again as long as I live. But I thought I would just try for once, and *see who was master.*"

The object of this little boy was to have his own will. He was not willing to submit to his mother, till he had tried his strength, to see whose will should prevail. He got a severe chastisement, and had to submit after all. And so it will always be with you, if you set out with the determination, if possible, always to have your own will. You will be always getting into difficulty, and gain nothing by it in the end.

III. The Affections. I shall not undertake in this place, to give a full and complete definition of the affections. It will answer my present purpose, to say that the *affections* are the *feelings* or *emotions of the heart*. This may not be philosophically accurate; but when my readers come, at a more advanced age, to study mental and moral philosophy, they can enlarge their views. For all practical purposes, this will answer.

And what I mean by *educating the affections* is, to acquire the habit of controlling the feelings, so as to suppress the bad and cultivate the good. You hear people talk of good and bad *dispositions*. But a good disposition is only the preponderance of good feelings; or in other words, where good feelings and good tempers prevail, we say, that person has a good disposition; but if bad feelings and evil tempers predominate, we say he has a bad disposition. There is, no doubt, a difference in natural dispositions. But with suitable efforts, and especially with the aid of God's grace, much may be done to cultivate and improve them.

With these preliminary remarks, I proceed to give some *rules for the cultivation* of the affections.

1. Check the first risings of Ill-temper.

The smith, who makes an edged tool, an axe, a knife, or any such instrument, first works the iron and steel into the form which he wishes, and then *tempers* it. While he is working it, he wants to keep it soft, so that he can work it easy; and this he does by keeping it hot. But after he gets it finished, he heats it in the fire, and dips it in water, so as to cool it suddenly, and that makes it hard. But, if he left it so, it would be so hard that it would break all to pieces as soon as it was used. So he holds it again over the fire, and heats it a little, to take out a part of the temper, and make it just of the hardness that he wishes. An instrument that is very hard is called *high-tempered;* one that is very soft is *low-tempered.* This is a good illustration of *temper* as it appears in us. A *high temper* is one that is easily excited, and that runs so high as to be in danger of doing great mischief. A *low temper* is a disposition easy and indifferent, like a knife tempered so little that the edge will turn the first time it is used. Now you want temper enough not to be indifferent, but not so much as to fly all in pieces. And I know nothing on which your usefulness and happiness more depend, than in the proper regulation of your temper; and not your own happiness alone, but the happiness of all around you. One of the first and greatest moral lessons is, to learn to control your temper. "He that is slow to anger," says Solomon, "is better than the mighty; and he that ruleth his spirit, than he that taketh a city." But "He that hath no rule over his own spirit, is like a city that is broken down and without walls." By indulging an ungoverned temper, you expose yourself to many evils. You show the weak points of your character, and lose the good opinion of others, and your own self-respect. You cannot help thinking meanly of yourself after having broken out in a sudden gust of anger, or given indulgence to a peevish, fretful spirit. To be ill-humoured, peevish, or cross, is to be unhappy, and to make others unhappy. But a sweet temper will not only make you happy, but like the balmy breezes of a summer evening,

it will shed a sweet fragrance all around you. Nothing
will render your character more unlovely than ill-temper;
nor, if habitually indulged at home, can it be concealed
even from the most careless observer. You will carry
the mark of it wherever you go. There will be the ill-
natured scowl, the knit brow, the distorted features,
which no sweet-scented soap can wash out, and no cos-
metic hide. It will spoil the most elegant features, and
mar the most beautiful countenance. But a sweet
temper will hide a thousand defects, and render the
most ordinary features beautiful and lovely. I do not
know any thing that adds a greater charm to the youthful countenance. But, if you would have a sweet
temper, you must suppress every ill-natured feeling;
never suffer yourself to be angry at trifles, nor get into
a storm of passion on any account: neither indulge a
peevish, fretful disposition; but, on the contrary, cultivate
and cherish *good-nature*, in every possible way. Strive
to be pleased with every thing around you, unless it is
positively bad; and never suffer the ill-humours of others
to disturb your own tranquillity. The noisy cataract
comes splashing its muddy waters over the side of the
mountain, leaping from rock to rock, now shouting, now
murmuring, now scolding, now rushing on in the wildest
fury, till it plunges into the great river; but the river
rolls quietly on its majestic way, undisturbed by the
babbling waterfall, which only makes a momentary ripple
upon the surface of its placid waters. But, suppose
the river should stop its course, to quarrel with the
noisy waterfall, what would be the consequence? The
whole country would be inundated with the fury of its
pent up waters. You cannot afford to get angry with
every one that is disposed to treat you ill. It costs too
much. Did you ever see a dog barking at the moon?
And what did the moon do? It went right straight on,

and minded nothing about it. The moon can't afford to stop and quarrel with the dog that barks at it.

"I know it is very foolish to be angry," perhaps you will say; "but how can I help it? I am suddenly provoked, and fall into a passion before I have time to think of it." The best remedy I can recommend is, that you make it a rule never to be angry till you have had time to consider whether you have any thing to be angry about. And, in making inquiry, do not ask whether the conduct that provoked you was bad; but, in the first place, try if you cannot find some apology for it, or some palliation; and, second, whether, admitting it to be as bad as it seems, it is really worth so great a sacrifice of feeling, on your part, as you will have to make, if you indulge your passions. And, among other considerations, ask yourself how this thing will appear a hundred years hence, when both yourself and the person who has provoked you, will be in eternity: "If I indulge my passions in this thing, shall I then be able to look back upon it with pleasure?" Some such reflections as these will tend greatly to cool your anger; and most likely, before you have thought upon the matter many minutes, you will conclude that is is not worth while to be angry.

So likewise, if you are given to fretfulness and ill-humour, consider whether there is any sufficient cause why you should thus make yourself miserable? And you will probably find that all your trouble is imaginary. Remember that every thing that concerns you is ordered by the providence of God; and think how much cause of thankfulness you have, every day, for his goodness. And what has he done that you should fret against him? He has perhaps suffered your will to be crossed; but he has done it for your good. Think, also, how this will appear a hundred years hence? "How will my fretfulness appear, when I look back upon it, from another world?" and if there were no sin in it, is there not much folly? For "why should I make myself miserable?"

2. NEVER GIVE THE LEAST INDULGENCE TO A JEAL-OUS OR ENVIOUS SPIRIT. To be *jealous*, is to suspect others of being unfriendly to us, or of a design to injure us. To be *envious*, is to be displeased with the prosperity of others, especially if they are likely to excel us. The effect of these two passions upon the disposition is very similar. If you are jealous of any person, you will be always looking for some evil design in his conduct; and your imagination will conjure up a thousand things that never had any existence, except in your own mind. This passion, habitually indulged, very often settles down into a kind of *monomania*, or partial insanity. I have known persons, whose im-aginings, through the influence of jealousy, became realities to their minds, and they would roundly assert as facts, the things that they had imagined respecting others. Such persons are perpetually in trouble, because they fancy some one is plotting against them. Your own comfort, therefore, depends on your suppressing the first motions of this evil affection. While you should be on your guard against imposition, and never confide implicitly in strangers, nor put yourself in the power of any one whose char-acter has not been proved; yet you should presume others to be friendly till they show themselves other-wise, and always give their conduct the best construc-tion it will bear.

Let me give you an example. There is Laura Williams: she is always in trouble, for fear some one does not like her. If any of her companions seem to take more notice of some other one than of herself, she begins to be jealous that their professions of friendship are not real; and if any one happens not to notice her for once, she considers it a slight; and so her feelings are perpetually disturbed. She is never happy. Sometimes she will weep, as if her heart would break, for some fancied slight; when, in reality, she has no occasion for trouble, and might just as well laugh as cry. She will be unhappy as long as she lives, and perhaps crazy before she dies, if she does not overcome this passion.

Envy is a more depraved passion than *jealousy;* but the effect upon the character is nearly similar. You will find a melancholy illustration of the nature and effects of envy, in the story of Haman, in the Book of Esther. Though exalted to the second place in the kingdom, he could not enjoy his elevation, so long as Mordecai the Jew sat in the king's gate. He could endure no rival.

But you will find examples enough of this passion among your own companions. There are those that cannot bear a rival; and if any of their companions excel themselves, they hate them. But consider how mean and ignoble such a feeling is. A truly generous spirit will rejoice in whatever is excellent, will love excellence wherever it appears; but a mean and selfish spirit would monopolize every thing to itself, and be offended, if excelled by others. Every noble sentiment revolts at the spirit of envy, so that this base passion always defeats itself. The envious person would be exalted above all; but envy debases him below all, and renders him despicable and miserable.

3. ACQUIRE THE HABIT OF REGARDING EVERY ONE WITH FEELINGS OF GOOD WILL. There are some persons who accustom themselves to look upon others with a critical eye, and seem to take pleasure in

detecting and exposing their failings. This leads to misanthropy; it makes people ill-natured. It leads them to look upon almost every one as an object of aversion. If this disposition begins in early life, and continues to be cultivated, it will grow and increase, till it settles at last into a sour, morose, malignant temper, that can never look with pleasure or satisfaction upon any human being.

Instead of indulging such a temper, you should look with feelings of *good-will* upon every one. Do not regard others with a critical eye. If they are not incorrigibly bad, so as to render them dangerous associates, overlook their faults, and study to find out some redeeming qualities. Consider that they belong to the same great family; that they are as good by nature as yourself; that they have immortal souls, to be saved or lost. Try what excuses or apologies you can find for their faults in the circumstances in which they have been reared. And though you may not see fit to make choice of them as your friends, yet *feel kindly towards them*. But especially, do not forget that you are not faultless yourself. This will exert a softening influence upon your own character; and you will find yourself much more happy in studying the good qualities of others, and exercising feelings of charity and good-will toward them, than you will in criticising and finding fault. The one course will make you amiable and happy; the other, unlovely and miserable.

4. Give free indulgence to every noble and generous sentiment. Rejoice when you see others prosperous. Why should you be unhappy, that another is more prosperous than yourself, if you are not injured by it? If you love your neighbour as yourself, his prosperity will be as grateful to you as your own. Rejoice, also, in the excellence of others. A truly

noble heart loves excellence for excellence's sake. A generous heart is forgetful of self; and when it sees excellence, it is drawn towards it in love. It would scorn to put little self between it and a worthy object.

This disposition should also be carried out in action. A generous and noble spirit will not always be contending for its own rights. It will yield rather than contend. Contention among companions and associates, for each other's rights, is a source of great unhappiness; and when it becomes habitual, as it sometimes does among brothers and sisters at home, it spoils the disposition. "That is *mine,*" says one. "No," says the other, "it is not yours, it is mine." And without waiting quietly to look into the matter, and investigate the question of right, they fall into a sharp contention. The matter in question was a mere trifle. It was not worth the sacrifice of *good-nature* which it cost. How much better both would feel, to keep good-natured, and give each other the reasons for their claims, and if they cannot agree, for one or the other to yield! Or, rather, how much more noble, if the contention be, which shall be allowed the privilege of yielding! There is more pleasure in one act of generosity than in all that can be enjoyed by selfish possession; and nothing will render you more lovely in the eyes of others than a noble and generous disposition.

5. BE GENTLE. Gentleness is opposed to all severity and roughness of manners. It diffuses a mild, bland, amiable spirit through all the behaviour. It has much to do with the cultivation of the affections. Where this is wanting, none of the amiable affections will flourish. A gentle spirit will show itself in a gentle behaviour, and a gentle behaviour will react upon the spirit, and promote the growth of all the mild and amiable affections. You can distinguish the

gentle by the motion of the head, or the sound of their footsteps. Their movements are quiet and noiseless. There is a charm in their behaviour which operates to secure for them the good opinion of all.

6. BE KIND. Every kind act that is performed, increases the kind feelings of the heart. If you treat your brothers and sisters kindly, you will feel more kindly towards them; while if you treat them with harshness and severity, or ill-treat them in any manner, it will seal up your affections towards them, and you will be more inclined to treat them with coolness and indifference. If you are habitually kind to every one, embracing every opportunity in your power to perform some office of kindness to others, you will find your good-will towards all increasing. You will be universally beloved, and every one will be kind to you. See that little girl! She has run back to assist her little brother, who has lost his shoe in the mud. How kindly she speaks to him, to soothe his feelings and wipe his tears! Some sisters that I have seen would have been impatient of the delay, and scolded him in a cross and angry manner for the trouble he made. But with a heart full of sympathy, she forgets herself, and is intent only on helping him out of trouble, and quieting his grief. But she has hardly got under way again, before she meets a little girl, who has just fallen down and spilled her berries, crying over her loss. Without once thinking of the trouble it would give her, she speaks kindly to the little girl, helps her to pick up the lost fruit, and then assists her to pick enough more to make up her loss. Every where she is just so, always glad of an opportunity to show kindness to every one she meets. And she gets her pay as she goes along. The happiness she feels, in thus being able to contribute to the comfort of others, is

far beyond any thing she could receive from mere selfish enjoyment. And, in addition to this, she gets the good-will of others, which makes them kind to her in return.

7. KEEP SELF OUT OF VIEW, AND SHOW AN INTEREST IN THE AFFAIRS OF OTHERS. This will not only interest others in you, but it will tend to stifle selfishness in your own heart, and to cultivate disinterested feeling. Sympathize with others; enter into their feelings; and endeavour, in heart and feeling, to make their interest your own, so that there may be a soil for disinterested feeling to grow in. If you see others enjoying themselves, rejoice with them. Make the case your own, and be glad that they have occasion to rejoice. "Rejoice with them that do rejoice." If you have truly benevolent feelings, it will certainly be an occasion of joy to you to see them prosperous and happy, whoever they are. On the other hand, sympathize with misery and distress. "Weep with them that weep." Wherever you see misery, let it affect your heart. And never fail, if it is in your power, to offer relief. And, often, you can afford the best relief to those of your own age, your companions, but especially your inferiors, by showing that you are affected with their troubles, that you sympathize with them. Cultivate the habit of *feeling* for others. When you see or read of the sufferings of the poor, when you read of the condition of the heathen, who know not the way of salvation, let your sympathies flow forth toward them. Learn to feel for others' woe, and it will improve your own heart. But, besides this, you will find yourself rewarded with the affections of others.

Thus I have given you a few brief hints, to show how the affections may be cultivated. I must leave you to apply them in practice to every-day life, and to carry out the principle, in its application to all the circumstances in which you may be placed; which principle is, as much as possible, to repress and refrain from exercising every bad feeling or affection, and to cherish and cultivate the good, bringing them into exercise on every fit occasion, that they may grow into habits.

You will see, by what I have said under the various heads of this chapter, that the idea of *educating the heart* is no mere *figure of speech*, but a reality, of great importance to your character and well-being through life. Your parents and teachers will, of course, pay attention to this matter; but they cannot succeed in it without your co-operation. And with you it must be an every-day work. You must carry it out in all your conduct and feelings, and seek the grace of God to aid you in so difficult a work. Without an *educated heart*, you will never be fit to fill the station designed for a WOMAN. A woman's excellence and influence *lie in the heart;* and no outward accomplishments can compensate for the want of a *good heart.*

Illustrations.

TEMPER AND TEAZING.

THERE was a rich nobleman in England, who had a little daughter named Anne. They were very fond of her; for she was a fine little creature, very lively and merry, affectionate, and exceedingly beautiful. But she had a naughty temper. When any thing vexed her, she would fly into a rage, and turn and strike any one that provoked her. After every fit of rage, she would be ashamed and sorry, and resolve never to be so bad again. But the next time she was provoked, it was all forgotten, and she was as angry as ever. When she was between four and five years of age, her mother had a little son, a sweet little tender baby. The servants, who were thoughtless and wicked, loved to teaze little Anne, because she was so easily irritated; and so they told her that her father and mother would not care for her now, because all their love and pleasure would be in this brother, and they would not mind her. Poor Anne burst into a flood of tears, and cried bitterly, saying, " You are a wicked woman to say so ; mamma will always love me, I know she will, and I'll go this very moment and ask her." And she darted out of the nursery, and flew to her mother's room. The servant called after her, " Come, Miss, you needn't go to your mother's room, she won't see you now." Anne burst open the door, but was instantly caught hold of by a strange woman she had never seen before. "My dear," said this woman, "you cannot be allowed to see your mamma just now," and she was going on to tell her that it was because she was very sick and must not be disturbed. But she was too angry to listen; and she screamed and kicked at the woman, who was obliged to take her by force and carry her back to the nursery. When she put her down, she gave the servant a charge to prevent her going to her mother's room. This added to her rage. But the wicked servant burst into a laugh, and said, "I told you that, Miss. You see your mamma does not love you now." The poor child became mad with fury. She seized a smoothing iron, and darting forward, threw it upon the baby's head, as it lay in the cradle. The child gave one struggle, and breathed no more.

Anne's mother died that night of grief. No other child was ever born to the family. Anne grew up and became the Countess of Crawford and Livingstone. She was fully informed of the fatal deed she had committed; and in all her life, was never afterwards known to smile.

This melancholy tale, which is a well-authenticated fact, teaches two important lessons: 1. The folly and danger of teazing children; and 2. The danger of indulging angry passions. When I see older people take delight in teazing children, or children in teazing one another, I think it an evidence of a bad disposition, a malicious, black heart. What else could give them delight in tormenting one another? And if I see a little girl in a storm of passion, her eye-balls flashing with rage, and her hands and feet flying with fury, I think of Cain, who killed his brother, and fear that some terrible disaster will happen. If any one of my readers is afflicted with a bad temper, I would advise her when she feels an angry fit coming on, to run to her room, as fast as her feet can carry her, and there remain till it is over, falling on her knees and praying God to give her strength to control it.

If any of you are tempted to teaze others, remember this sad story, and reflect what consequences followed the thoughtless conduct of these vicious servants who amused themselves by exciting the passions of this little girl. But if any one teazes you, think what a slave you make of yourself, by suffering your temper to be disturbed by such things. Have independence enough not to mind what is said on purpose to teaze you; and then no one will attempt it. These servants by teazing, and this girl by being teazed, were both guilty of murder; and the lives of the mother and the child were both lost in consequence.

CONSCIENCE.

CONSCIENCE is the faculty which distinguishes between right and wrong, and approves or condemns us, according as we do one or the other. It is a generous friend, but a terrible enemy; and, if we would keep its friendship, we must be careful to do nothing to offend it. The following story not only illustrates the power of conscience to accuse and condemn, but likewise shows the importance of being strictly honest in little things. Girls, who rob their mothers' closets of cakes and sweetmeats, and boarding-school misses, who peculate upon the larder or the baker's basket, may see to what they are exposing themselves. These are dangerous practices. When habitually indulged, they blunt the

conscience in regard to the rights of others, and sometimes produce the confirmed habit of thieving. This
woman suffered more than tongue can tell, from having
indulged this thievish habit at boarding-school.

In the year 1835, a lady about thirty-eight years of
age, elegantly dressed, entered the shop of a pastry-
cook in the neighbourhood of London, in great mental
excitement, and inquired if Mr. B. was still alive, as
she wished to see him. The man was engaged, and
sent his daughter, to whom she stated, that more than
twenty years before, she was at a boarding-school, which
Mr. B. supplied with pastry; and that while there, she
was in the habit of taking little articles from his tray,
unknown to the person who brought it. She had now
been married some years, and was the mother of six
children, having every comfort which this world could
afford; but the remembrance of these petty thefts so
haunted her conscience that she was never happy. Her
husband, perceiving that she was unhappy, inquired the
cause; and finding it continued to prey upon her spirits,
he advised her to see if the pastry cook was alive, and
to make him or his family a recompence; and as she
was about to leave London that day, she had come
for that purpose. After begging his forgiveness, she
insisted on his accepting a sum of money, which she
believed to be about the value of the articles stolen.

CHAPTER XV.

THE term MIND is often employed to signify all the faculties of the soul. But I shall use it in application to the *intellectual faculties*, in distinction from the *moral;* as I have employed *heart* to denote the *moral*, in distinction from the *intellectual.* I shall not undertake to give a strictly philosophical distinction of the mental faculties, but shall comprehend them in the following division, which is sufficient for my purpose, to wit: *Perception, Reason or Understanding, Judgment, Memory,* and *Imagination.* PERCEPTION is the faculty that receives ideas into the mind; as, when you look at a tree, immediately the idea of a tree is impressed on the mind through the sense of sight; or, when you touch an object, the idea of that object is impressed on your mind through the sense of touch; or, you may receive the idea of a spirit, from the explanations which you hear or read.

The REASON, or UNDERSTANDING, is the faculty that considers, analyzes, and compares ideas received into the mind, and forms conclusions concerning them. For example, suppose you had never seen a watch: one is presented to you, and, as soon as your eye rests upon it, you form an idea respecting it. Perhaps this idea is no more than that it is a very curious object. But, immediately, your understanding is employed in *considering* what it is, the perceptive faculty still being occupied in further discoveries. From the fact that there is motion, you conclude there must be some *power* within it; for motion is not produced without power. Here is *consideration* and *conclusion,* which is a regular operation of reason. But, to make further discoveries, you open the watch, to examine its parts. This is *analyzing.* You examine all the parts that you can see, on removing the case. You still see *motion,* all the wheels moving in regular order; but the *cause* of the motion, the *power* that moves, is yet unseen. You perceive a chain wound round a wheel, and attached to another wheel, around which it is slowly winding itself; and this chain appears to regulate the whole movement. You conclude that the power must be in this last-named wheel. Here is a conclusion from analyzing, or examining the parts separately.

The JUDGMENT is the same as what is popularly styled *common sense.* It is that faculty which pronounces a decision, in view of all the information before the mind, in any given case. For example, if you wish to determine what school you will attend, you first obtain all the information you can respecting the different schools that claim your attention. You consider and compare the advantages of each; and you decide according to your impression of their comparative merits. The faculty which forms this decision is called the *judgment.* You will readily perceive how very important this faculty is; for a person may be very learned, and yet a very great *dunce* in every thing of a practical nature, if he fails in judgment or common sense. His learning will be of very little use to him, because he has not sense to use it to advantage.

The MEMORY is the faculty which *retains* the knowledge that is received into the mind. It is a wonderful faculty. It may be compared to an immense closet, with a countless number and variety of shelves, drawers, and cells, in which articles are stored away for future use, only one of which can be examined by the proprietor at the same time, and yet so arranged that he knows just where to look for the article he wants. It is supposed that no impression, once made upon the memory, can be obliterated; and yet the impression may not be called up for years. It lies there, till some association of ideas brings it up again; the faculty not being able to present more than one object distinctly before the mind at the same instant.

The IMAGINATION is that faculty which forms pictures in the mind of real or unreal scenes. It is the faculty that you exercise in your fanciful plays, and when your mind runs forward to the time that you expect to be engaged in the busy scenes of life, and you picture to yourself pleasures and enjoyments in prospect. It is the faculty chiefly exercised by the poet and the writer of fiction.

You will, perhaps, be tired of this explanation ; but it was necessary, in order to prepare the way for what I have to say on the *education of the mind.* From the definition of education already given, you will perceive that my ideas differ very much from those entertained by most young people. Ask a young person what he is going to school for, and he will answer, " *To learn.*" And his idea of learning is, simply, to *acquire knowledge.* This, however, is but a small part of the object of education. And this idea often leads youth to judge that much of what they are required to study is of no value to them; because they think they shall have no use for the particular science they are studying, in practical life. The chief objects of mental education are, to cultivate and discipline the mind, and to store it with those great facts and principles which compose the elements of all knowledge. The studies to be pursued, then, are to be chosen with reference to these objects, and not merely for the purpose of making the mind a vast storehouse of knowledge. This may be done, and yet leave it a mere lumber-room. For without the capacity to analyze, and turn it to account, all the knowledge in the world is but useless lumber. It is of great importance that young people should understand and appreciate this principle, because it is intimately connected with their success in acquiring a good education. To this end, it is necessary that they should co-operate with their parents and teachers. This they will never be ready to do, if they suppose the only object of study is, to acquire a knowledge of the particular branches they are set to learn; for they cannot see the use of them. But, understanding the design of education to be to discipline the mind, and furnish it with the elements of knowledge, there is no science, no branch of learning, but what is useful for these objects; and the only question, where education cannot be liberal, is, What branches will best secure these ends?

This understanding of the objects of education is also necessary, to stimulate the young to prosecute their studies in the most profitable manner. If their object were merely to acquire knowledge, the more aid they could get from their teachers the better, because they would thus obtain information the more rapidly. But the object being to discipline the mind, call forth its energies, and obtain a thorough knowledge of elementary principles, what is *studied out*, by the unaided efforts of the pupil, is worth a hundred times more than that which is communicated by an instructor. The very effort of the mind which is requisite to study out a sum in arithmetic, or a difficult sentence in language, is worth more than it costs, for the increased power which it imparts to the faculties so exercised. The principles involved in the case will, also, by this effort, be more deeply impressed upon the mind. Such efforts are also exceedingly valuable, for the confidence which they inspire in one's power of accomplishment. I do not mean to commend self-confidence in a bad sense. For any one to be so confident of his own power as to think he can do things which he cannot, or to fancy himself qualified for stations which he is not able to fill, is foolish and vain. But, to know one's own ability to do, and have confidence in it, is indispensable to success in any undertaking. And this confidence is inspired by unaided efforts to overcome difficulties in the process of education. As an instance of this, I recollect when a boy, of encountering a very difficult sum in Arithmetic. After spending a considerable time on it, without success, I sought the aid of the school teacher, who failed to render me any assistance. I then applied to several other persons, none of whom could give me the desired information. Thus I was thrown back upon my own resources. I studied upon it several days without success. After worrying my head with it one evening, I retired to rest, and *dreamed* out the whole process. I do not suppose there was any thing supernatural in my dream; but the sum was the absorbing subject of my thoughts, and when sleep had closed the senses, they still ran on the same subject. Rising in the morning with a clear head, and examining the question anew, it all opened up to my mind with perfect clearness; all difficulty vanished, and in a few moments the problem was solved. I can scarcely point to any single event, which has had more influence upon the whole course of my life than this. It gave me confidence in my ability to succeed in any reasonable undertaking. But for this confidence, I should never have thought of entering upon the most useful undertakings of my life. But for this, you would never have seen this book, nor any other of the numerous works which I have been enabled to furnish for the benefit of the young. I mention this circumstance here, for the purpose of encouraging you to *independent mental effort*. In prosecuting your studies, endeavour always, if possible, to overcome every difficulty without the aid of others. This practice, besides giving you the confidence of which I have spoken, will give you a much better knowledge of the branches you are pursuing, and enable you, as you advance, to proceed much more rapidly. Every difficulty you overcome, by your own unaided efforts, will make the next difficulty less. And though at first you will proceed more slowly, your habit of independent investigation will soon enable you to outstrip all those who are still held in the leading-strings of their teachers. A child will learn to walk much sooner by being let alone, than to be provided with a go-cart. Your studies, pursued in this manner, will be much more interesting; for you are interested in any study just in proportion to the effort of mind it costs you.

The *perceptive faculty* is developed first of all. It begins to be exercised by the child before it can speak, or even understand language. *Reason* and *judgment* are more slow in their development, though they begin to be exercised at a very early period. *Memory* is exercised as soon as ideas are received into the mind. The *imagination*, in the natural course of things, is developed latest of all; but it is often forced out too early, like flowers in a hot-bed, in which case it works great injury to the mind.

You will perceive the great importance of bringing out the several faculties of the mind in their due proportion. If the *memory* is chiefly cultivated, you will have a great amount of knowledge floating loosely in your mind, but it will be of very little use. But the proper cultivation of the memory is indispensable, in order to render your knowledge available. Nor will it do for you to adopt the notion that nothing is to be committed to the keeping of the memory which is not fully understood. The memory is a *servant*, which must consent to do some things without knowing the reason why. The *imagination* is the beautiful flower that crowns the top of the plant. But if forced out too early, or out of due proportion, it will cover the stalk with false blossoms, which, in a little time, will wither, and leave it dry and useless. The *perception, reason, and judgment*, require a long course of vigorous exercise and severe training, in order to lay a solid foundation of character.

I shall leave this subject here, without suggesting any particular means of cultivating the mind, leaving you to apply the principles here laid down to your ordinary studies. But in several subsequent chapters, I shall have some reference to what I have said here.

Illustrations.

No one knows what changes may take place in her situation. The eyes are a very delicate structure, easily destroyed. The ears are often gradually closed, and the mind shut up in silence. Then the soul is dependent upon *memory* for its intellectual food. Happy, at such times, are they that have their minds stored with the precious word of God. A young lady was led into the presence of an eminent surgeon, totally blind and deaf. This calamity came upon her suddenly, by a violent pain in the head. She was brought to be examined, to see whether there was any relief. Several surgeons were present, all of whom pronounced her case hopeless. After this was over, and she was taken to the house of a friend, she eagerly inquired what the doctor said, and whether he could afford her any relief. The only way her inquiries could be answered was, by tapping her hand for " *No*," and squeezing it for " *Yes*," for she could not hear the loudest noise, nor distinguish day from night. When she received the answer " No," she burst into tears, and wept aloud, in the bitterness of despair. "What! shall I never again see the light of day, nor hear a human voice? Must I remain incapable of all social intercourse, shut up in silence and darkness while I live?" Again she wept. The scene was truly affecting. Had she been able to *see*, she might *read*, and receive the sympathetic expression of the countenances of her friends. Had she been only blind, she could receive knowledge and expressions of friendship through the sense of hearing. But both these avenues were closed, to be no more opened in this world. Her friends could pity, but could not relieve. And to add to the trial, she was an orphan, with no father, mother, brothers, or sisters, to pity and care for her. She was entirely dependent upon a few pious friends for support. This she keenly felt. As she continued to weep, a friend took up a Bible and placed it on her breast. She felt it, and said, "Is this the Bible?" She was answered that it was. She held it to her bosom, and said, --This is the only comfort I have left, though I shall never be able to read it any more," and began to repeat some of its promises, as "Cast thy burden on the Lord, and he will sustain thee." "As thy day is, so shall thy strength be." " Call upon me in the day of trouble, and I will deliver thee." "My grace is sufficient for thee." " In a moment," says the narrator, "she dried her tears, and became one of the happiest creatures I ever saw." She never seemed to deplore her condition afterwards. Although the channels of communication with the world were closed, one was opened between her soul and heaven. When she was a very little girl, she had been to the Sabbath School, where she had committed to memory many portions of Scripture; and these were the manna on which her soul now feasted.

3

THE ASSEMBLY'S CATECHISM.

In a certain school district in the State of New York, there lived a man who was an infidel, and bitterly opposed to religion. The Assembly's Catechism was taught in the district school; but when the children were called upon to recite it, this man's children were placed on a seat by themselves, and forbidden to take part in the exercise. They went home grieved that they should be treated so differently from the rest of the children, and asked their mother what it meant. She told them she did not know, though she suspected the cause. When her husband came home, she told him about it, and asked him whether, as she suspected, it was by his orders. He told her it was. He had forbidden the instructer of the school to teach it to them. "Then," said the mother, "they shall learn it at home." "No," said he, "they shall never learn it at home. I will never have it brought into the house." "I have the catechism, every word of it, in my heart," she replied; "and as long as I am your wife, I shall teach it to our children." The man said no more, but went to the teacher, and said, "My wife is queen, and you must teach the catechism to the children." This woman had committed the whole catechism perfectly to memory, when a child.

Another woman, when she became very old and blind, so that she could not read, took great comfort in repeating the catechism, every word of which she remembered; and she dwelt with great delight on the precious truths which it contains.

HYMNS.

Many years ago, several German families left their native land and settled in this country. Among them was a man from Wirtemberg, who settled with his family in Pennsylvania. There were no churches or schools in that part of the country; and he was obliged to keep the Sabbath with his family at home, instructing them to read the Bible and pray, and to commit to memory portions of Scripture and hymns.

In the year 1754, a terrible war broke out between the French and English. The Indians took part with the French; and some of them came into Pennsylvania, murdering the inhabitants and burning their houses. They reached the dwelling of the family from Wirtemberg, while the mother and one of the sons were gone to a mill, four miles distant, to get some corn ground. The father, the eldest son, and two little girls named Barbara and Regina, were at home. The father and son were instantly killed; but the little girls were carried away into captivity, with a great many other children, who were taken in the same manner. They were led many miles, through woods and thorny bushes, that no body might follow them.

Barbara was at this time ten years old, and Regina nine. It was never known what became of Barbara; but Regina, with a little girl whom she had never seen before, was given to an old Indian woman, who was very cruel to them. Her only son lived with her, and maintained her; but he was sometimes from home for weeks together, and then these poor little children were forced to go into the woods to gather roots and other things for the old woman to eat; and when they did not bring her enough, she would beat them so cruelly that they were nearly killed. And now Regina began to find the advantage of committing to memory Scripture, Hymns, and Prayers. She would kneel down with the other little girl, under a tree, and repeat the prayers to the Lord Jesus, and the hymns, which her father had taught her; and the little girl prayed with her, and learned the prayers and hymns by heart. In this condition these children remained nine long years, till Regina was nineteen, and her little companion eleven years old. While captives, they took much comfort in repeating together the verses and hymns which Regina's father had taught her. They would cheer each other, especially with one hymn from the German hymn-book, used at Halle, in Germany:

"Alone, yet not alone am I,
    Though in this solitude so drear."

They constantly hoped that the Lord Jesus would sometime bring them back to their Christian friends. In the year 1764, this hope was realized. The English Colonel Bouquet came to the place where they were, conquered the Indians, and made them restore all their prisoners. More than four hundred were brought to him, and among others, these two little girls. The Colonel and his soldiers gave them food and clothes, and brought them all to the town of Carlisle, in Pennsylvania, and published a request in the newspapers that all parents, who had lost their children, would come to this place, and see if they could find them among the captives. Regina's mother came, but her child had become a stranger to her. Regina had the language and manners of the Indians, and neither mother nor daughter knew each other. The poor mother went up and down among the young captives, but could find nothing of her daughters. She wept in bitter grief and disappointment. Colonel Bouquet asked her if she recollected nothing by which her children might be discovered. She said she recollected nothing but the following hymn, which she used to sing with them:

" Alone, yet not alone am I,
    Though in this solitude so drear;
I feel my Saviour always nigh,
    He comes, the weary homes to cheer.
I am with him and he with me,
Even here alone I cannot be."

He requested her to sing the hymn; but she had scarcely sung two lines of it, when Regina rushed from the crowd, began to sing too, and flew into her mother's arms. They both wept for joy. But the other sister was not found, and no one came for the other little girl, Regina's companion, who clung to her and would not let her go. Regina's mother, though poor, took them both home with her. Regina repeatedly asked her mother for " the Book in which God speaks to us;" for she remembered that, when her father took down the Bible to read to them he always said, " Now, my children, be still, and listen to what I am going to read; for it is God who speaks to us in this book." But her mother had no Bible. She lost ever thing when the Indians burnt their house. She determined to go to Philadelphia and buy one: but the pastor of the church, learning her situation, gave her a Bible. Regina had not forgotten what her father had taught her; for she was able to read the Bible, as soon as she received it.

Thus the hymns and Scriptures which this young woman had learned when she was a little girl, besides being a great comfort to her in her long captivity, were the means of restoring her to her mother.

CHAPTER XVI.

READING occupies a very important place in education. It is one of the principal means of treasuring up knowledge. It is, therefore, highly necessary that a taste for reading should be early cultivated. But a mere *taste for reading*, uncontrolled by intelligent principle, is a dangerous appetite. It may lead to ruinous consequences. The habit of reading *merely for amusement*, is a dangerous habit. *Reading for amusement* furnishes a constant temptation for reading what is injurious. It promotes, also, an *unprofitable manner* of reading. Reading in a hasty and cursory manner, without exercising your own thoughts upon what you read, induces a bad habit of mind. To profit by reading depends, not so much on the *quantity* which is read, as upon the *manner* in which it is read. You may read a great deal, in a gormandizing way, as the glutton consumes food, and yet be none the better, but the worse for what you read.

If you would profit by reading, you must, in the first place, be careful *what you read*. There are a multitude of books, pamphlets, periodicals, and newspapers, in circulation at the present day, which cannot be read, especially by the young, without great injury, both to the mind and heart. If any one should propose to you to associate with men and women of the lowest and most abandoned character, you would shrink from the thought, you would be indignant at the proposition. But it is not the mere bodily presence of such characters that makes their society dangerous. It is the communion which you have with their minds and hearts, in their conduct and conversation. But a great portion of the popular literature of the day is written by such characters. By reading their writings, you come into communion with their minds and hearts, as much as if you were personally in their company. In their writings, the fancies which fill their corrupt minds, and the false and dangerous principles which dwell in their depraved hearts, are transferred to paper, to corrupt the unwary reader. Here are, likewise, glowing descriptions of evil conduct, more fascinating to the youthful heart than the example itself would be, because the mischief is artfully concealed behind the drapery of fine literary taste, and beautiful language. There are, likewise, many such writings, the productions of persons of *moral lives*, but of *corrupt principles*, which are equally dangerous. You would not associate with a person whom you knew to be an unprincipled character, even though he might be outwardly moral. He would be the more dangerous, because you would be less on your guard. If it is dangerous to keep company with persons of bad character or bad principles, it is much more so to keep company with bad books. I shall here suggest, for the regulation of your reading, a few simple rules.

1. ALWAYS HAVE SOME DEFINITE OBJECT IN VIEW, IN YOUR READING. While pursuing your education, you will be so severely taxed with hard study, that reading merely for diversion or amusement does not furnish the

relaxation which you need. It keeps the body idle and the mind still in exercise; whereas, the diversion which you need, is something that will exercise the body and relax the mind. If your object is *diversion*, then it is better to seek it in useful labour, sprightly amusements, or healthful walks. I can think of nothing more injurious to the young than spending the hours in which they are released from study, bending over novels, or the light literature of our trashy periodicals. Not only is the health seriously injured by such means, but the mind loses its vigour. The high stimulus applied to the imagination creates a kind of mental intoxication, which renders study insipid and irksome. But reading is an important part of education, and some time should be devoted to it. Instead of mere amusement, however, there are higher objects to be aimed at. These are, 1st, to store the mind with useful knowledge; 2nd, to cultivate a correct taste; 3rd, to make salutary impressions upon the heart. For the first, you may read approved works on all the various branches of knowledge; as history, biography, travels, science, and religious truth. For the second, you may read such works of imagination and literary taste as are perfectly free from objection, on the score of religion and morality, and these but sparingly at your age; for the third, such practical works of piety as you will find in the Sabbath School library. But, for all these purposes, the *Bible* is the great Book of books. It contains history, biography, poetry, travels, and doctrinal and practical essays. Any plan of reading will be essentially defective, which does not contemplate the daily reading of the Bible. You ought to calculate on reading it through, in course, every year of your life.

2. Be exceedingly careful what you read. Do

not take up a book, paper, or periodical, that happens to fall in your way, because you have nothing else to read. By so doing, you will expose yourself to great evils. But, though a book be not decidedly objectionable, it may not be *worth reading*. There are so many good books, at the present day, that it is not worth while to spend time over what is of little value; and it is better to read the Bible alone, than to spend time over a poor book. Avoid, especially, the fictitious stories that you will find in newspapers and popular magazines. They are generally the worst species of fiction, and tend strongly to induce a vitiated taste, and an appetite for novel-reading. If you once become accustomed to such reading, you will find it produce a kind of *moral intoxication*, so that you will feel as uneasy without it, as the drunkard without his cups, or the smoker without his pipe. It is much the safer way for young people to be wholly directed by their parents, (or their teachers, if away from home,) in the choice of their reading. Make it a rule never to read any book, pamphlet, or periodical, till you have first ascertained from your parents, teachers, or minister, that it is safe, and worth reading.

3. THINK AS YOU READ. Do not drink in the thoughts of others as you drink water; but examine them, and see whether they carry conviction to your own mind; and if they do, think them over, till they become incorporated with your own thoughts, part and parcel of your own mind. Lay up facts and principles in your memory. Let the beautiful thoughts and striking ideas that you discover be treasured up as so many gems and precious stones, to enrich and beautify your own mind. And let your heart be impressed and benefited by the practical thoughts you find addressed to it.

4. REDEEM TIME FOR READING. Although it would be improper for you to take the time appropriated for study, or to rob yourself of needful diversion, yet you may, by careful economy, save some time every day for reading. A great deal of time is thrown away by the indulgence of dilatory habits, or consumed in a careless, sauntering vacancy. If you follow system, and have a time for every thing, and endeavour to do every thing with despatch, in its proper season, you will have time enough for every thing that is necessary to be done.

Illustrations.

DR. JOHNSON'S OPINION OF NOVELS.

DR. JOHNSON one day called upon Garrick, the play-actor, and was shown into his study to wait for his appearance. In an adjoining room were all the novels and other light works, which had been presented to Mr. Garrick by his friends. The door being open, Dr. Johnson went in, and taking up first one and then another of the books, read a little, and threw it down. Before Garrick arrived, the floor was strewed with these splendid volumes. Garrick was very angry at finding Johnson there, and said it was a private cabinet, and no company was admitted there. "But," said Johnson, "I was determined to examine some of your valuables, which I find to consist of three sorts: *stuff*, *trash*, and *nonsense*."

NOVELS AND PLAYS.

AT a dinner party of young gentlemen, some years ago, in Philadelphia, theatrical performances were spoken of with great approbation, and praised as the best *moral* school in the world. One of the company being silent, his opinion was asked. He begged leave to differ from them entirely; and gave it as his opinion that such performances were calculated to check in young gentlemen and ladies, all solid moral and mental improvement, and to introduce extravagance, dissipation, and light and frivolous conversation. This fixed the eyes of the whole company upon him, with a sternness that convinced him that they thought his opinion deserved the strongest disapprobation. But to convince them that he was right, he proposed that they should appoint a committee of two of their number, with whom he would visit the theatre two or three nights in a week for a month, on condition that they should the next morning introduce him to some of the young gentlemen and ladies who were at the play. This was agreed to. At the expiration of a month, the same party dined together, in order to hear the report of their committee; who stated that of eighty young ladies, whom they had visited the next morning after the play, only one of them had spoken of the *moral* of the play; and that the conversation was generally respecting the dresses and gestures of the actors and actresses, the fashionable dresses of the ladies in the audience, novels, dances, etc. This conversation had convinced the committee that plays and novels were a very great injury to all solid improvement, and this report convinced the whole company of the correctness of the gentleman's opinion at the previous party.

THE FOLLY OF ROMANCE.

NOVEL-READING fills the heads of young girls with romantic notions. They become weary with the dull round of ordinary life. They sigh for some *adventure*, such as they have read of in works of fiction. The restless and uneasy spirit thus cultivated prepares them to become an easy prey to the false-hearted libertine.

A young lady of sixteen, an orphan, under the care of an uncle, was attending a boarding-school in Upper Canada. She was delicately bred, and ignorant of the world. Her naturally romantic feelings had doubtless been fostered by the pernicious practice of novel-reading, which has turned the heads of thousands. A man was introduced to her friends as a gentleman of standing and respectability; and, by his pleasing address and winning manners, soon presented to her mind the *beau-ideal* of the romance. He proposed marriage. Her guardian and other friends opposed it. He was a stranger. She was too young. But this opposition was necessary to complete the romance, and make out an *adventure*. An elopement was now agreed upon. They ran away together, and were married in Detroit. It was not long, however, before he was overtaken by a creditor, from the place where he had formerly resided, arrested, carried to Cleveland, Ohio, and put in jail. His young and beautiful wife followed him, declaring herself willing to die with him in prison. This was necessary to complete the romance. But then she was informed that he had left a *wife* as well as *creditors*, at the East. The scene was now heart-rending. All the romantic hopes, which for weeks had filled her mind, were now dashed in a moment. The fiend in human shape, who had deceived her, being released from prison, left her to her fate. For him she had given up all; the home and companions of her childhood, her guardian and friends; and now he not only abandons her, but denies their marriage. She returned, ashamed and broken-hearted, to her friends: a lesson to romantic girls not to make matches in their teens, against the advice of their friends: a lesson to boarding-school misses to mind their studies, and keep shy of novels, men, and boys.

READING IN THE NIGHT.

GIRLS sometimes contract the habit of reading in bed, with a lamp by their side; or of sitting up late, to read, after they have retired to their rooms.   Either of these practices is both injurious and dangerous.   It is a good thing to have a taste for reading; but the day, in summer, and the day and early part of the evening, in winter, are long enough to do every thing that needs to be done.   "The night cometh, when no man can work." The night is for rest and repose.   No one can safely encroach upon it.   The habit, of which we are speaking, has ruined the eyes of many a girl for life; and in many instances, she has dropped asleep, and left her light burning, which has caught the bed-clothes or the furniture of the room, and set the house on fire.

Tirzah Locke had acquired this dangerous habit. There was nothing she loved so well to do, as to sit up late at night to read, after all others in the house had retired to rest.   She would undress, and put on her night-clothes, wrap a large blanket round her, and recline herself, in the most comfortable position, in a large easy chair, by the side of the table which held her lamp; and there she would sit and read, perhaps half the night.   Two or three times she fell asleep there, and slept till morning, when she found her lamp still burning, or the oil burned out. One night Mr. Williams, with whom she lived, was called up to prepare some medicine for his wife; and, as he opened the door, he thought he perceived a smoke. He went up stairs and opened the door where his daughters slept, and one or two other doors, when he hastened to Tirzah's room. The smoke rushed out, so that he was obliged to step back to get his breath. But in a moment he returned and opened the window. The smoke was so thick that he thought Tirzah could not live there long; and he went to the bed, but she was not there. At that moment there was a blaze near the table, which discovered her, lying in the large chair, surrounded by flames, and apparently suffocated. Mr. Williams caught her in his arms, and carried her down stairs. The family were roused, and with some difficulty the fire was put out. On searching for the cause, it appeared that Tirzah had fallen asleep while reading, and, in her sleep, had thrown out her arms towards the light, with the book in her left hand; for the book, which was a beautiful annual that had been given her by her mother, was nearly consumed. There was a large place burned in the top of the table, a small place in the floor, and the whole covering of the chair. Tirzah was stifled, almost beyond recovery; and it was a long time before she could be revived. Then she was almost delirious, in view of the consequences of her carelessness, and her narrow escape. She was sick a number of days.

Some years after, she sat in an open window, with a fan and a glass in one hand, and the other moving cautiously over the branch of a rose-bush, which grew so near the window as to enter the room, when the window was raised. She had just been trying to distinguish the colours of some flowers; but they seemed to be all blended and indistinct. The habit which she indulged while a girl, of reading late at night, though she perceived no ill effects at the time, had ruined her sight; and she was destined to spend the remainder of her days in almost total darkness.

CHAPTER XVII.

WRITING.

WRITING, or COMPOSING, is one of the best exercises of the mind. It is, however, I am sorry to say, an exercise to which young people generally show a great aversion. One reason, perhaps, is, that, to write well, requires *hard thinking*. But I am inclined to think the chief reason is, that the difficulties of writing are magnified. There is, also, a want of wisdom in the choice of subjects. Themes are frequently selected for first efforts, which require deep, abstract thinking; and the mind not being able to grasp them, there is a want of thought, which discourages new beginners. The first attempts should be made upon subjects that are easy and well understood; such as a well-studied portion of history, a well-known story, or a description of some familiar scene; the object being to clothe it in suitable language, and to make such reflections upon it as occur to the mind. Writing is but *thinking on paper;* and if you have any thoughts at all, you may commit them to writing.

Another fault in young beginners is, viewing composition as a *task* imposed on them by their teachers, and making it their chief object to cover a certain quantity of paper with writing; and so the sooner this

3

task is discharged the better. But you must have a higher aim than this, or you will never be a good writer. Such efforts are positively injurious. They promote a careless, negligent habit of writing. One well-written composition, which costs days of hard study, is worth more, as a discipline of mind, than a hundred off-hand careless productions. Indeed, one good successful effort will greatly diminish every succeeding effort, and make writing easy. You will do well, then, first to select your subject some time before you write, and think it over and study it, and have your ideas arranged in your mind before you begin. Then write with care, selecting the best expressions, and clothing your thoughts in the best dress. Then carefully and repeatedly read it over, and correct it, studying every sentence, weighing every expression, and making every possible improvement. Then lay it aside a while, and afterwards copy it, with such improvements as occur at the time. Then lay it aside, and after some days revise it again, and see what further improvements and corrections you can make, and copy it a second time. If you repeat this process half a dozen times, it will be all the better. Nor will the time you spend upon it be lost. One such composition will conquer all the difficulties in the way of writing; and every time you repeat such an effort, you will find your mind expanding, and your thoughts multiplying, so that, very soon, writing will become an easy and delightful exercise; and you will, at length, be able to make the first draught so nearly perfect that it will not need copying. But you never will make a good writer by off-hand careless efforts.

Letter-writing, however, is a very different affair. Its beauty consists in its simplicity, ease, and freedom from formality. The best rule that can be given for letter-writing is, to imagine the person present whom you are addressing, and write just what you would say in conversation. All attempts at effort, in letter-writing, are out of place. The detail of particulars, such as your correspondent would be interested to know, and the expression of your own feelings, are the great excellencies of this kind of writing. Nothing disappoints a person more than to receive a letter full of fine sentiments, or didactic matter, such as he might find in books, while the very information which he desired is left out, and perhaps an apology at the close for not giving the news, because the sheet is full. In a letter, we want *information of the welfare of our friends*, together with the warm gush of feeling which fills their hearts. These are the true excellencies of epistolary writing.

CHAPTER XVIII.

THERE is no greater enemy to improvement than an indolent spirit. An aversion to effort paralyzes every noble desire, and defeats every attempt at advancement. If you are naturally indolent, you must put on resolution to overcome it, and strive against it with untiring vigilance. There is not a single point, in the process of education, at which this hydra-headed monster will not meet you. "The slothful man saith, There is a lion without, I shall be slain in the street." There is always a lion in the way, when slothful spirits are called upon to make any exertion. "*I can't*," is the sovereign arbiter of their destiny. It prevents their attempting any thing difficult or laborious. If required to write a composition, they *can't* think of any thing to write about. The Latin lesson is difficult; this word they *can't* find; that sentence they *can't* read. The sums in arithmetic are *so hard*, they *can't* do them. And so this lion in the way defeats every thing. But those who expect ever to be any thing, must not suffer such a word as *can't* in their vocabulary.

It is the same with labour. The indolent dread all exertion. When requested to do any thing, they have something else to do first, which their indolence has left unfinished; or they have some other reason to give why they should not attempt it. But if nothing else will do, the sluggard's excuse, "*I can't,*" is always at hand. Were it not for the injury to them, it would be far more agreeable to do, one's self, what is desired of them, than to encounter the painful scowls that clothe the brow, when they think of making an effort. Solomon has described this disposition to the life: "The slothful man putteth his hand in his bosom: *it grieveth him to take it out again.*"

But indolence is a source of great misery. There are none so happy as those who are *always active.* I do not mean that they should give themselves no relaxation from severe effort. But relaxation does not suppose *idleness.* To sit and fold one's hands, and do nothing, serves no purpose. Change of employment is the best recreation. And from the idea of employment, I would not exclude active and healthful sports, provided they are kept within due bounds. But to sit idly staring at vacancy is intolerable. There is no enjoyment in it. It is a stagnation of body and mind. An indolent person is, to the active and industrious, what a stagnant pool is to the clear and beautiful lake. Employment contributes greatly to enjoyment. It invigorates the body, sharpens the intellect, and promotes cheerfulness of spirits; while indolence makes a torpid body, a vacant mind, and a peevish, discontented spirit.

Indolence is a great waste of existence. Suppose you live to the age of seventy years, and squander in idleness one hour a day, you will absolutely throw away about three years of your existence. And if we consider that this is taken from the waking hours of the day, it should be reckoned six years. Are you

willing, by idleness, to shorten your life six years?
Then take care of the moments.   Never fritter away
time in doing nothing.   Whatever you do, whether
study, work, or play, enter into it with spirit and
energy; and never waste your time in sauntering and
doing nothing.   "Whatsoever thy hand findeth to do,
do it with thy might; for there is no work, nor device,
nor knowledge, nor wisdom, in the grave, whither
thou goest."

CHAPTER XIX.

ON DOING ONE THING AT A TIME.

WHAT is worth doing at all, is worth the undivided attention; but Julia can never be satisfied to do but one thing at a time. By attempting to read or play while dressing, she consumes double the time that is necessary. She reads at the table, and, in consequence, keeps the table waiting for her to finish her meal. She turns her work into play, and thus her work is slighted, and frequently left half done. When she goes to her lesson, her attention is arrested by something else before she has fairly commenced, and she stops to look or listen. Or perhaps she insensibly falls into a reverie, and is engaged in building "castles in the air," till something happens to call back her spirit from the fairy land. The consequence is, the lesson is acquired but imperfectly, while twice the needful time has been spent upon it. At the same time, nothing else is accomplished. This is what I call *busy idleness*.

The true way to accomplish the most, and to do it in the best manner, is to confine the attention strictly to the thing in hand, and to bend all the energies of the mind to that one object, aiming to do it in the best possible manner, in the least possible time. By adopting this principle, and acting upon it, you will be surprised to find how much more expeditiously you will accomplish what you undertake, and how much better it will be done. It is indispensable to success in any undertaking.

Closely connected with this subject, is the *systematic division of time.* Where there is no system, one duty will jostle another, and much time will be wasted in considering what to do next; all of which would be avoided, by having a regular routine of duties, one coming after the other in regular order, and so having a set time for each. This cannot be carried out perfectly, because there will every day be something to do that was not anticipated. But it may be so far pursued as to avoid confusion and waste of time.

CHAPTER XX.

BEGINNING things and leaving them unfinished, exerts a bad influence in the formation of character. If it becomes a habit, it will make you so fickle that no one will put confidence in you. There is Jane Henderson. If you go into her room, you will find her table strewed, and her drawers filled, with compositions begun and not completed; scraps of verses, but no poem finished; a dozen letters begun, but not one completed; bits of lace commenced, and laid aside; a dozen different squares of patch-work begun, but not one full square among them all. She wants energy and perseverance to finish what she begins; and thus she wastes her time in frivolous pursuits. She is very ready to *begin;* but before she has completed what is begun, she thinks of something else that she wishes to do; or she grows weary of what she is upon, and so leaves it, and tries something else. She lives to no purpose, for she *completes* nothing; and she might as well *do nothing,* as *complete nothing.*

If you indulge this practice, it will grow upon you, till you will become weak, irresolute, fickle, and good for nothing. To avoid this, begin nothing that is not worth finishing, or that you have not good reason to think you will be able to finish. But when you have begun, resolutely persevere till you have finished. There is a strong temptation, with the young, to abandon an undertaking, because of the difficulties in the way; but, if you persevere, and conquer the difficulties you meet with, you will gain confidence in yourself, and the next time, perseverance in your undertakings will be more easy.   You may, however, make a mistake, and begin what you cannot or ought not to perform; in which case, perseverance would only increase the evil.

CHAPTER XXI.

CHOICE OF SOCIETY, AND FORMATION OF FRIENDSHIPS.

CHARACTER is formed under a great variety
of influences. Sometimes a very trifling circumstance gives direction to the whole course of one's
life. And every incident that occurs, from day to
day, is exerting a silent, gradual influence, in the formation of your character. Among these influences,
none are more direct and powerful than that exerted
upon us by the companions with whom we associate; for we insensibly fall into their habits. This
is especially true in childhood and youth, when the
character is plastic, like soft wax, easily impressed.

But we cannot avoid associating, to some extent,
with those whose influence is injurious. It is necessary, then, for us to distinguish society into *general*
and *particular*. General society is that with which
we are *compelled to associate*. Particular society is
that which we *choose for ourselves*. In school, and in
all public places, you are under the necessity of
associating somewhat with all. But those whom you
meet, in such circumstances, you are not compelled to
make intimate friends. You may be courteous and
polite to all, wherever and whenever you meet them,
and yet maintain such a prudent reserve, and cautious

deportment, as not to be much exposed to contamination, if they should not prove suitable companions.

But every one needs *intimate friends;* and it is necessary that these should be well chosen. A bad friend may prove your ruin. You should therefore be slow and cautious in the formation of intimacies and friendships. Do not be suddenly taken with any one, and so enter into a hasty friendship; for you may be mistaken, and soon repent of it. There is much force in the old adage, " All is not gold that shines." A pleasing exterior often conceals a corrupt heart. Before you enter into close intimacies or friendships, study the characters of the persons whom you propose to choose for companions. Watch their behaviour and conversation; and if you discover any bad habits indulged, or any thing that indicates a want of principle, let them not become your companions. If you discover that they disregard any of the commandments of God, set them down as unsafe associates. They will not only be sure to lead you astray, but you can place no dependence upon their fidelity. If they will break one of God's commands, they will another; and you can put no confidence in them. But even where you discover no such thing, ask the opinion of your parents respecting them before you choose them as your friends. Yet, while you are in suspense about the matter, treat them courteously and kindly. But when you have determined to seek their friendship, do not impose your friendship on them against their will. Remember that they have the same right as yourself to the choice of their friends; and they may see some objection to the formation of a friendship with yourself. Be delicate, therefore, in your advances, and give them an opportunity to *come half way.* A friendship cautiously and slowly formed will be much more likely to last than one that is formed in haste.

But let the number of your intimate and confidential friends be small. It is better to have a few select, choice, and warm friends, than to have a great number, less carefully chosen, whose attachment is less warm and ardent. But you must not refuse to associate at all with the mass of the society where you belong; especially, if you live in the country. You must meet them kindly and courteously, on all occasions where the society in general in which you move is called together. You must not affect exclusiveness, nor confine yourself to the company of your particular friends, at such times. But be careful that you do not expose yourself to evil influences.

You ought not, at present, to form any intimate friendships with the other sex. Such friendships, at your age, are dangerous; and if not productive of any serious present evils, they will probably be subjects of regret when you come to years of maturity; for attachments may be formed that your judgment will then disapprove.

CHAPTER XXII.

NATURE abounds with profusion of ornament. The trees of the forest are crowned with beauty. The flowers of the field are arrayed in the most gorgeous combination of beautiful colours, surpassing the imitation of man. The bowels of the earth enclose the richest gems; and even its dens and caverns are garnished with beautiful workmanship, far exceeding the highest achievements of art. The animate creation, also, displays the same love of beauty. The wild beasts are arrayed in the richest furs. The fowls of the air, and even the serpent that crawls on the earth, are adorned with a profusion of rich and beautiful colours. And man, the crowning work of the Creator, is adorned with symmetry of shape and beauty of features. But, above all, the mind itself has one entire faculty for ornament. The imagination is the flower of the mind, which crowns the intellectual tree with beauty and glory.

The voice of nature, therefore, forbids us to banish ornament from our systems of education. But equally does the same voice forbid us to make ornament the chief end of education. It is neither the *beginning* nor *end* of it. The rose does not grow on the root of the tree; nor does the plant, at its first growth, display its gorgeous colours. The trunk of the tree, the stem of the plant, the branches and the leaves, all precede the flower. Those are the *substantials,* this is the *ornament.* The former must be matured before the latter can appear. So, likewise, the substantial parts of education must take precedence of the ornamental. And the flower itself is not merely nor mainly for *beauty;* but it is *in order to fruit.* So the ornamental branches of education, in their proper places, are to be pursued with an eye to usefulness. However, the flower must be a long time budding before it blooms; and so may the ornamental branches of education be commenced and pursued a long time before they arrive at such perfection as to display their beauty, or discover their usefulness.

The solid branches, then, are to occupy the first place, and receive the chief attention. But the ornamental branches, at their proper time and in their proper places, are not to be neglected. Young people, however, are inclined to give them an undue importance, and disposed to pursue them to the neglect of that which is solid and substantial. David compared the daughters of Jerusalem to "corner stones, polished after the similitude of a palace." But the stones must be quarried and beaten out into the proper shape, before they can be *polished.* Polishing is the last work. This shows the place that is to be given to ornamental education. No one can receive an ornamental education merely. There must first be a solid superstructure; after which comes the polish. There are, however, some ornamental branches, which need to be pursued a long time, before they arrive at any degree of perfection. Such are music, drawing, and painting. They cultivate particular faculties; and this cultivation must necessarily be slow in its progress. Music, as a science, is perhaps as useful a discipline of mind as any other study. The cultivation of the voice and of the ear, is also of great importance. So, also, is the skilful use of the fingers, in playing on instruments; which is much more easily acquired in childhood than at any other period of life.

Drawing and painting cultivate the eye, and impart a quick perception of beauty. They also give the power of transferring to paper the image imprinted on the mind through the sense of sight. These branches are not merely ornamental, but often highly useful.

A good education is that process by which all the faculties and powers of the mind are developed in due proportion. That is a one-sided education which cultivates highly some particular faculties, while it neglects others. Such a mind will be deformed and out of proportion. To produce a well-balanced mind, the solid parts of education must receive the chief attention, because they constitute the very foundation of character. But it is a great mistake to conclude that they are all that is necessary, especially for females. By an exclusive attention to the solid branches, and that in a high degree, the character is rendered too masculine. There is need of the softening influence of those pursuits which are designed chiefly to embellish. And this should not be forgotten, in the pursuit of letters.

The imagination and the taste should be cultivated, within proper bounds, so as to give symmetry of character.

Taste is, perhaps, not a distinct faculty by itself, but rather a combination of the faculties, concentrating them upon an object, and giving a nice and quick perception of beauty or deformity. It is exercised with respect to language, in discerning its correctness and beauty, or its incorrectness and deformity, without any process of reasoning or any comparison with rules of grammar or rhetoric. In a similar manner, it detects and points out, at a glance, the beauty or the deformity, the excellences or defects, of a picture or a landscape, or whatever object it beholds. This faculty, or combination of faculties, is cultivated by the study of music, drawing, painting, etc., with respect to the eye and ear; and in the study of language, with respect to the conceptions of the mind, and the manner of expressing them. I know of nothing, in the whole process of education, which contributes more to personal enjoyment than the cultivation of a correct taste. It also greatly recommends one to the regard of others. And, if chastened with piety, it may contribute to devotional feeling, by increasing our admiration of the beauties of creation, and through them leading us to adore the wisdom of the Creator.

3   O

CHAPTER XXIII.

ON AMUSEMENTS.

THE human system is formed for alternate labour and rest, and not for incessant activity; and to provide for this, the night follows the day, and the Sabbath the six days of labour. But not only is rest necessary after labour, but activity in a different direction. When you are carrying a burden of any kind, you find relief in a change of position. A poor boy was employed in turning a wheel, by which he was enabled to do something for his mother. A lady, observing him steadily employed at what appeared to be a very laborious occupation, inquired whether he did not get tired. He replied that he was often very tired. "And what do you do when you are tired?" she further inquired. "O," said he, "I take the other hand." He had learned that a change of position gave him rest. Neither the mind nor the body is capable of being incessantly exerted, in one direction, without injury. Like the bent bow, they will lose their elasticity. The body, after labour, and the mind, after study, need unbending, especially in youth, while the muscles of the body have not acquired maturity or solidity, and the powers of the mind are yet developing. At this period of life, relaxation and amusement are especially necessary;

and those young persons who eschew all play, and confine themselves to books and labour, must, in the natural course of things, suffer both in health and spirits. Healthful play is natural to the young, throughout the whole animal creation. The lamb, that emblem of innocence, is seen sporting in the fields, blithely bounding over the hills, as if desirous of expressing a grateful sense of its Creator's goodness. There is no more harm in the play of children than in the skipping of the lambs. It is necessary to restore the bent bow to its natural elasticity. It is the voice of nature, which cannot be hushed.

But having said so much, it is necessary to guard against improprieties and excesses in amusements. And yet, to determine what amusements are to be allowed, and what condemned, is no easy matter; for, while some kinds of amusement are evil in their own nature, and necessarily injurious, others are evil and injurious only on account of their *excess*, or of the *manner* in which they are pursued, or of the evils that are associated with them. My object is, not so much to point out what amusements are wrong, as to give you some rules by which you can judge for yourself.

1. Never engage in recreation at an *unsuitable time*. To neglect *duty* for the sake of amusement is not only wrong, but it will exert a bad influence upon your character. It tends to produce an immoderate love of amusement, and to break up all orderly and regular habits. Let your invariable rule be, "BUSINESS FIRST, AND THEN PLEASURE." Never suffer any kind of amusement to break in upon the time appropriated to labour or study.

II. Never do any thing that is *disapproved by your parents* or *guardians*. They desire your happiness, and will not deprive you of any enjoyment, unless they see good reason for it. They may see evil where you would not perceive it. They regard your highest welfare. They look beyond the present, to see what influence these things will have on your character and happiness hereafter. They are also set over you of the Lord; and it is your duty not only to submit to their authority, but to reverence their counsel.

III. Engage in no amusement which is *disapproved by the most devoted and consistent Christians* of your acquaintance. I do not mean the few *cross* and *austere* persons, who always wear an aspect of gloom, and cannot bear to see the countenances of youth lighted up with the smile of innocent hilarity. But I mean those Christians who wear an aspect of devout cheerfulness, and maintain a holy and consistent life. Their judgment is formed under the influence of *devotional feeling*, and will not be likely to be far from what is just and right.

IV. Do nothing which you would be *afraid God should see*. There is no darkness nor secret place, where you can hide yourself from his all-searching eye. Contemplate the Lord Jesus Christ as walking by your side, as he truly is in spirit; and do nothing which you would be unwilling that he should witness, if he were with you in his bodily presence.

V. Do nothing, the preparation for which *unfits you for religious duty*. If an amusement in which you are preparing to engage so takes up your mind as to interfere with your devotional exercises; if your thoughts run away from the Bible that you are reading to anticipated pleasures; or if those pleasures occupy your thoughts in prayer; you may be sure you are going too far.

VI. Engage in nothing on *which you cannot first ask God's blessing*. Do you desire to engage in any thing in which you would not wish to be blessed and prospered? But God only can bless and prosper us in any undertaking. If, therefore, your feelings would be shocked to think of asking God's blessing on any thing in which you would engage, it must be because your conscience tells you it is wrong.

VII. Engage in no amusement which *unfits you for devotional exercises.* If, on returning from a scene of amusement, you feel no disposition to pray, you may be sure something is wrong. You had better not repeat the same again.

VIII. Engage in nothing which *tends to dissipate serious impressions.* Seriousness, and a sense of eternal things, are perfectly consistent with serenity and cheerfulness. But thoughtless mirth, or habitual levity, will drive away such impressions. Whatever you find has this effect is dangerous to your soul.

IX. Reject such amusements as are generally *associated with evil.* If the influences which surround any practice are bad, you may justly conclude that it is unsafe, without stopping to inquire into the nature of the practice itself. Games of chance are associated with gambling and dissipation; therefore, I conclude that they cannot be safely pursued, even for amusement. Dancing, also, is associated with balls, with late hours, high and unnatural excitement, and dissipation; it is therefore unsafe. You may know the character of any amusement by the company in which it is found.

X. Engage in nothing which necessarily *leads you into temptation.* You pray every day, (or ought to,) "Lead us not into temptation." But you cannot offer up this prayer sincerely, and then run needlessly in the way of temptation. And if you throw yourself in the way of it, you have no reason to expect that God will deliver you from it.

XI. If you engage in any recreation, and return from it with a *wounded conscience*, set it down as evil. A clear conscience is too valuable to be bartered for a few moments of pleasure; and if you find your conscience accusing you for having engaged in any amusement, never repeat the experiment.

XII. Practise no amusement which *offends your sense of propriety*. A delicate sense of propriety, in regard to outward deportment, is in manners what conscience is in morals, and taste in language. It is not any thing that we arrive at by a process of reasoning, but what the mind as it were instinctively perceives. It resembles the sense of taste; and by it one will notice any deviation from what is proper, before he has time to consider wherein the impropriety consists. There is a beauty and harmony in what is proper and right, which instantly strikes the mind with pleasure. There is a fitness of things, and an adaptation of one thing to another, in one's deportment, that strikes the beholder with sensations of pleasure, like those experienced on beholding the harmonious and beautiful blending of the seven colours of the rainbow. But when *propriety* is disregarded, the impression is similar to what we might suppose would be produced, if the colours of the rainbow crossed each other at irregular angles, now blending together in one, and now separating entirely, producing irregularity and confusion. The sensation produced upon the eye would be unpleasant, if not insufferable. Among the amusements which come under this rule are the vulgar plays that abound in low company, especially such as require the payment of forfeits, to be imposed by the victor. In such cases, you know not to what mortification you may be subjected. *Frolics,* in general, come under this head, where rude and boisterous plays are practised, and often to a late hour of the night, when all sense of propriety and even of courtesy is often forgotten.

XIII. Engage in nothing of *doubtful propriety*. The apostle Paul teaches that it is wrong to do any thing, the propriety of which we doubt; because, by doing, that which we are not fully persuaded is right, we violate our conscience. It is always best to keep on the safe side. If you were walking near the crater of a volcano, you would not venture on ground where there was any danger of breaking through, and falling into the burning lake. You would keep on the ground where it was safe and sure. And so we should do, in regard to all questions of right and wrong. *Never venture where the ground trembles under your feet.*

XIV. Do nothing which you will *remember with regret on your dying bed.* It is well always to keep death in view; it has a good effect upon our minds. The death-bed always brings with it pains and sorrows enough. It is a sad thing to make work for repentance at such an hour. That is an honest hour. Then we shall view things in their true light. Ask yourself, then, before entering into any scene of amusement, how it will appear to you when you come to look back upon it from your dying bed.

XV. Do nothing in the midst of which you would be *afraid to meet death.* When preparing for a scene of pleasure, how do you know but you may be cut down in the midst of it? Sudden death is so common, that it is folly to be in any place or condition in which we are not prepared to meet it. Many persons have been cut down in the midst of scenes of gayety, and the same may occur again. A man in Germany was sitting at the gaming table. His card won a thousand ducats. The dealer handed over the money, and inquired how he would continue the game. The man made no reply. He was examined, and found to be a corpse! Similar scenes have occurred in the ball-room. In the midst of the merry dance, persons have been called suddenly out of time into eternity. A gentleman and lady started in a sleigh, to ride some distance to a ball, in a cold winter's night. Some time before reaching the place, the lady was observed to be silent. On driving up, the gentleman called to her, but no answer was returned. A light was procured, and he discovered, to his amazement, that he had been riding with a corpse! At no moment of life are we exempt from sudden death. He who holds us in his hand has a thousand ways of extinguishing our life in a moment. He can withhold the breath which he gave; he can stop the vital pulsation instantly; or he can break one of the thousand parts of the intricate machinery of which our mortal bodies are composed. No skill can provide against it. We ought not, therefore, to trust ourselves, for a single moment, in any place or condition where we are unwilling to meet death.

XVI. Do nothing for which you will be *afraid to answer at the bar of God.* There every secret thing will be revealed. What was done in the darkness will be judged in open day. "Rejoice, O young man, in thy youth; and let thy heart cheer thee in the days of thy youth; and walk in the ways of thine heart, and in the sight of thine eyes: but know thou that for all these things God will bring thee into judgment." A young man, on leaving home to enter the army, was supplied with a small Bible, which, though a thoughtless youth, he always carried in his pocket. On one occasion, after a battle, he took out his Bible, and observed that there was a bullet hole in the cover. His first impulse was, to turn over the leaves, and read the verse on which the ball rested. It was the passage just quoted. It brought before his mind all the scenes of mirth and sinful pleasure in which he had been engaged, and pressed upon him the fearful truth, that for all of them he was to be brought into judgment. It was the means of awakening him to a sense of his condition, and led to a change of heart and life. And why should not the same solemn impression rest upon your mind, with respect to all scenes of pleasure, and lead you carefully to avoid whatever you would not willingly meet at that awful tribunal?

If you apply these tests to the various amusements that are in vogue among young people, you may readily discern what you can safely pursue, and what you must sternly reject. It will lead you, especially, to detect the evils of all theatrical performances, balls, cards, and dancing parties, country frolics, and all things of a like nature. But it will not deprive you of one innocent enjoyment. A girl, ten or twelve years old, made a visit to a companion about her own age. Both of them were hopefully pious. On returning home, she told her mother she was sure Jane was a Christian. "Why do you think so, my daughter?" inquired the mother. "O," said the daughter, "*she plays like a Christian.*" In her diversions she carried out Christian principles, and manifested a Christian temper. This is the true secret of innocent recreation; and it cuts off all kinds of amusement that cannot be pursued in a Christian-like manner.

Illustrations.

DANCING

A PIOUS lady had two children, a son and a daughter. The son was immoral in his conduct, and a source of great grief to his mother; but the gentle and docile character of the daughter gave great promise of excellence. She grew up beautiful and graceful; and her father, who was not a pious man, insisted on sending her to the village dancing school. To the mother, who had devoted her child to God, such an act seemed little short of sacrilege. But, in spite of her tears and entreaties, the daughter was decorated with the earnings of the doating father, and sent to this school of fashion and folly. Her beauty was so remarkable, and her natural graces so attractive, that she soon became the belle of the village.

The father now died, and the poor widow was enabled to withdraw her daughter from these scenes of temptation. She sought, with some success, to instruct her in those religious truths, which had proved her own comfort and support in scenes of trial. The daughter lent a willing ear, and seemed to be the subject of good impressions; and two years after the death of her father, she was on the point of making a public profession of religion. But now the village was thrown into great excitement. Some rich men, to show their *generosity*, determined to gratify the people with a *horse-race* and a *ball*. The poor widow shuddered as she witnessed the rapid progress of this much dreaded evil. In the midst of this excitement, her deceased husband's brother came to town with his only daughter, and stopped at her house. This man was a horse-jockey, and his daughter an ardent votary of second-hand fashions and graces. He fell into raptures at the sight of his niece's beauty, and declared that he would be at the expense of equipping her like his own child, and that she should eclipse all the women of rank and fashion in the ball-room.

The poor girl was at first unwilling to listen to these follies; but she had always delighted in dancing, and, on this occasion, suffered her better judgment to be overruled. "Tis but for once, mother," said she, "and to please my uncle, nay, to avoid giving him incurable offence. Believe me, I shall not suffer my head to be turned by one night of gaiety. Pray for me, mother, that this compliance with the will of my father's brother may not produce evil consequences."

"My child," said the distressed mother, "I dare not so word my supplication. It is in compliance with *your own will*, that you thus venture on the tempter's own ground, and in this open act of disobedience to your Heavenly Father I cannot lend my aid to excuse or extenuate your guilt. I have prayed, I will still pray that you *may not* venture still further in this matter; but if you do, the responsibility must rest with yourself."

"But, mother, the Scriptures say there is a 'time to dance.'"

"So, they say, in the same place, 'there is a time to make war, a time to hate.' The wise man means that all sins and follies will have their seasons, but he does not, therefore, advocate sin and folly. O beware, my child, and let the same Scriptures tell you, that he who hardeneth his neck under reproof shall be destroyed, and *that suddenly*. These are fearful words, my child. O heed my reproof, and do not harden your neck."

"Mother," the girl replied, "I have promised my uncle to go to this unlucky ball, and I cannot break my promise without offending him. He has been so kind that it would seem ungrateful to disappoint him in this trifle."

"O my daughter," said the mother, stopping her ears, "let me not hear you use such awful language! Can it be *you* who call this sin a trifle! Go, if you will, but make no more vain attempts to make it appear right, lest you add to your condemnation."

The daughter went to the ball. She was much admired, and so often solicited to dance that her blood became painfully overheated. She started to go to a little back porch, in order to find relief from the heated atmosphere of the room. As she was passing rapidly out of the room, she met a servant, half intoxicated, carrying a pitcher of water. In staggering out of the way he overset the water into her bosom. This sudden shock was too much for her. It brought on a violent ague, which terminated in convulsions, and before the dawn of day, she expired in the arms of her distracted mother. She was heard, in her last moments, with difficulty to utter the word *"suddenly,"* evidently alluding to the warning which her mother had given her.

This narrative affords a good answer to the question, whether it is safe for girls to attend the dancing-school. If they learn to dance, they will then be importuned to go to balls; and we have seen how this young lady overcame her scruples. We cannot disregard the hand of God in her sad end; but if we could, and there were no *moral* evils attending such places of amusement, the danger to health and life, to which young ladies are exposed, by these unnatural excitements, heated rooms, stimulating refreshments, and exposure to the cold while heated, is a sufficient reason why they should not attend. But the exposure to *moral evils* is still greater. The ball-room is the place to harden the heart against all serious impressions. It is the place where the unwary are exposed to the most dangerous seductions. It is the place where no one can expect the grace of God to help her to resist temptation.

A CONTRAST TO THE FOREGOING.

THERE was a young girl, who was beloved by very many friends, and whose warm heart reciprocated all the affections which were bestowed upon her. She had a father and mother, who were extensively known and respected. She had brothers and sisters, both older and younger than herself; and love was the presiding genius of the family. The mother was a pious woman, and she faithfully instructed her children in their duty to God. The daughter of whom we are speaking, was early brought, as she believed, to receive the blessed Saviour as her friend and the guide of her youth. Soon after, she left home to attend school. Though here she met a large number of the gay and thoughtless, she turned away from those who wasted the precious time allotted them for improvement in vain and trifling amusements. After some months, she returned home, and soon after united with the Church.

Arrangements were then made for her to spend several months in the city; and a short time before she left home, her father, who was a man of the world, told her that it was his wish that she should spend part of her time in attending the *dancing-school*, for the purpose of *polishing her manners!* As though good manners could only be learned in the school of vanity and folly. But nothing that this father could have done, would have given greater pain to his beloved child than this request. She was anxious to please and honour him; but she thought a compliance with his wishes would dishonour the Saviour, to whom she had just devoted herself. She told her father how she felt; and her mother approved her choice. But her father laughed at what he called her folly, and turned away from her with displeasure. She was grieved to the heart. She loved her father; but she loved her Saviour more. She retired to her closet. and like good king Hezekiah, "spread the matter before the Lord." She prayed earnestly that He who has power to change the heart, would reconcile her father to the decision which she had made. She returned to the parlour. Her father's feelings were softened, though he knew not what she had been doing. In tones of tenderness, he said, "My child, I will not insist upon your attending the dancing-school. If you prefer not to attend it, you shall act your pleasure."

These words from her father, so different from those which he had so recently addressed to her, filled her with sweet peace. She went to the city, where she entered a school of sixty young ladies, all older than herself, and all gay and thoughtless. When they went to the dance, she went to the prayer-meeting or the social circle. She did not seclude herself, but enjoyed the society of some of the most refined and intellectual people in the city: a far better school for the improvement of manners, than a company of thoughtless young people, under the direction of an unprincipled Frenchman, to teach them how to hop and skip scientifically and gracefully. This young lady has lived many years, and passed through a great variety of scenes and changes; but she has never regretted the decision which she made at that time. How much better the termination, in this case, than in the other, where the young girl went to dancing-school to please an ungodly father, and to a ball to please a worldly-minded uncle, and from the ball-room, to eternity!

DEATH IN A BALL-ROOM.

A student was spending a vacation with a celebrated physician. On a beautiful but keenly cold evening in January, a young gentleman came into the office, and with a hurried air, inquired for the doctor. As the physician was not to be found, the student was requested to go with the young man, which he did. On the way, the young man informed him that there was a ball at the hotel, which had been interrupted by the sudden illness of one of the belles of the evening. On arriving at the hotel, they were surprised at the rapid filling and driving away of the carriages. The hilarity of the occasion had been suddenly exchanged for mute terror. Hurrying through the crowd, they entered the ball-room. It was spacious and brilliantly lighted, but deserted of its occupants, save a horror-stricken group in the centre. On a sofa, which had been drawn from the side of the room, sat a young lady, in a stooping posture, as though in the act of rising, with one hand stretched out to take that of her partner, who was to have led her to the dance. With the smile upon her lip, and eyes beaming with excitement, death had seized her. The smile of joy was now transformed to a hideous grin. The beaming eye now seemed but a glazed mass, protruding from the socket. The carmine added to give brilliancy to her complexion, now contrasted strangely with the sallow hue her skin assumed, while the gorgeous trappings, in which fashion had decked her, seemed but a mocking of the habiliments of the grave. The pale mother, as she knelt beside her child, groaned out, "Not here! not here! Let her die at home!"

I do not pretend to say that God sends death into the ball-room to show his disapprobation of such scenes. This would not be a fair conclusion; for death sometimes seizes people in the house of God. We do not know the reasons of God's providential dispensations; though open and presumptuous sins are often visibly punished. As I have remarked before, the exposure, the tight dressing, and the high excitement of the ball-room, has a strong tendency to bring on sudden death, especially with females. It may be, also, that God intends by it to show that no place is exempt from the destroyer. At all events, the fact that so many have been suddenly called into eternity from such scenes of mirth, shows that it may occur again; and *who would wish to die in a ball-room?*

CHAPTER XXIV.

GOVERNMENT OF THE TONGUE.

THE apostle James says, the *tongue* is an unruly member, and that it is easier to control a horse or a ship, or even to tame wild beasts and serpents, than to govern the tongue. And, though a very little member, it is capable of doing immense mischief. He even likens it to a fire. A very small spark, thrown into a heap of dry shavings, in a wooden house, in a great city, will make a terrible fire. It may burn up the whole city. So a very few words, carelessly spoken by an ungoverned tongue, may set a whole neighbourhood on fire. You cannot, therefore, be too careful how you employ your tongue. It is of the highest importance to your character and usefulness, that you early acquire the habit of controlling this unruly member. For the purpose of aiding you in this, I shall give a few simple rules.

RULES FOR GOVERNING THE TONGUE.

1. *Think before you speak.* Many persons open their mouths, and set their tongues a-going like the clapper of a wind-mill, as though the object was, to see how many words could be uttered in a given time,

3

without any regard to their *quality;* whether *sense* or *nonsense,* whether good, bad, or indifferent. A tongue, trained up in this way, will never be governed, and must become a source of great mischief. But accustom yourself, before you speak, to consider whether what you are going to say is worth speaking, or whether it can do any mischief. If you cultivate this habit, your mind will speedily acquire an activity, that will enable you to make this consideration without waiting so long before answering your companions as to be observed; and it will impose a salutary restraint upon your loquacity; for you will find others often taking the lead of conversation instead of yourself, by seizing upon the pause that is made by your consideration. This will be an advantage to you, in two ways. It will give you something better to say, and will diminish the *quantity.* You will soon perceive that, though you say less than some of your companions, your words have more weight.

II. *Never allow yourself to talk nonsense.* The habit of careless, nonsensical talking, is greatly averse to the government of the tongue. It accustoms it to speak at random, without regard to consequences. It often leads to the utterance of what is not strictly true, and thus insensibly diminishes the regard for truth. It hardens the heart, and cherishes a trifling careless spirit. Moreover, if you indulge this habit, your conversation will soon become silly and insipid.

III. *Do not allow yourself in the habit of* JOKING *with your companions.* This tends to cultivate severe sarcasm, which is a bad habit of the tongue. And, if you indulge it, your strokes will be too keen for your companions to bear; and you will lose their friendship.

IV. *Always speak the truth.* There is no evil habit, which the tongue can acquire, more mischievous and wicked than that of speaking falsehood. It is in itself very wicked; but it is not more wicked than mischievous. If all were liars, there could be no happiness; because all confidence would be destroyed, and no one would trust another. It is very offensive to God, who is a *God of truth*, and who has declared that all liars shall have their part in the lake that burns with fire and brimstone. It is a great affront and injury to the person that is deceived by it. Many young persons think nothing of deceiving their companions, in sport; but they will find that the habit of speaking what is not true, even in sport, besides being intrinsically wrong, will so accustom them to the utterance of falsehood, that they will soon lose that dread of a lie which used to fortify them against it. The habit of exaggeration, too, is a great enemy to truth. Where this is indulged, the practice of uttering falsehood, without thought or consideration, will steal on insensibly. It is necessary, therefore, in detailing circumstances, to state them accurately, precisely as they occurred, in order to cultivate the habit of truth-telling. Be very particular on this head. Do not allow yourself so little an inaccuracy, even, as to say you laid a book on the table, when you put it on the mantel, or on the window-seat. In relating a story, it is not necessary that you should state every minute particular, but that what you do state should be exactly and circumstantially true. If you acquire this habit of accuracy, it will not only guard you against the indulgence of falsehood, but it will raise your character for truth. When people come to learn that they can depend upon the critical accuracy of whatever you say, it will greatly increase their confidence in you. But if you grow up with the habit of speaking falsehood, there will be very little hope of your reformation, as long as you live. The character that has acquired an habitual disregard of truth is most thoroughly vitiated. This one habit, if indulged and cherished, and carried with you from childhood to youth, and from youth upwards, will prove your ruin.

V. Remember that *all truth is not to be spoken at all times.* The habit of uttering all that you know, at random, without regard to times and circumstances, is productive of great mischief. If you accustom your tongue to this habit, it will lead you into great difficulties. There are many of our own thoughts, and many facts that come to our knowledge, that prudence would require us to keep in our own bosom, because the utterance of them would do mischief.

VI. *Never, if you can possibly avoid it, speak any thing to the disadvantage of another.* The claims of justice or friendship may sometimes require you to speak what you know against others. You may be called to testify against their evil conduct in school, or before a court of justice; or you may be called to warn a friend against an evil or designing person. But, where no such motive exists, it is far better to leave them to the judgment of others and of God, and say nothing against them yourself.

VII. *Keep your tongue from tale-bearing.* There is much said in the Scriptures against tattling. "Thou shalt not go up and down as a tale-bearer, among the children of thy people." "A tale-bearer revealeth secrets." "Where no wood is, the fire goeth out; and where there is no tale-bearer, the strife ceaseth." Young people are apt to imbibe a taste for neighbourhood gossip, and to delight in possessing family secrets, and in repeating personal matters and neighbourhood scandal. But the habit is a bad one. It depraves the taste and vitiates the character, and often is the means of forming for life the vicious habit of tale-bearing.

And tale-bearers, besides the great mischief they do, are always despised, as mean, mischievous, and contemptible characters.

If you will attentively observe and follow the foregoing rules, you will acquire such a habit of governing the tongue, that it will be an easy matter; and it will give dignity and value to your character, and make you beloved and esteemed, as worthy the confidence of all.

Illustrations.

THE WASHERWOMAN.

SCARCELY is there a habit of more mischievous tendency than tattling. It is a vice to which females have peculiar temptations; and it is generally supposed to prevail more among them than among the other sex. But, whether this be true or not, we have an example of a woman in humble life, which shows that *a woman can govern her tongue*. In a small town there lived a woman, who supported herself more than forty years by washing for people at their houses; and all this time, *she was never known to repeat in one house what was said in another*. It is hardly necessary to say that she gave perfect satisfaction to her employers. In several instances, she was employed for the whole forty years in the same families. This example is worthy the imitation of all; but especially of those who are employed, as many young females are in this country, in dress-making, house-work, or other services, in different families in the same neighbourhood. It is in their power to do great mischief; and they have a strong temptation to it. But they have, also, a good opportunity to learn the very difficult art of governing the tongue.

JENNY JENKINS.

A TALE-BEARER is always despised by the whole neighbourhood. Solomon says, "Where no wood is the fire goeth out; and where no tale-bearer is, strife ceaseth." One tale-bearer can easily set a whole village on fire. And yet, though it does so much mischief, and destroys their own reputation, many girls love to tell tales, as well as they love to eat cakes and sweet-meats. Jenny Jenkins was a sad tattler. Every thing she heard, she told over and over again, without giving herself the least trouble in the world to find out whether it was true or not. Indeed, she often added to the story; for tale-bearers are rarely satisfied with the plain unvarnished truth.

WHISPERERS.

"A WHISPERER separateth chief friends." Prov. 16, 28.

A *whisperer* is one who slily insinuates things to the disadvantage of others; who tells tales secretly, and charges those to whom she pretends to be revealing secrets, to tell nobody. But very likely, the next person she meets will hear the same story, perhaps with a little more exaggeration, and accompanied with the same charge not to tell any body. Thus, in a few hours, the whole village will have the news, under strict injunctions of secrecy. But, often this gossiping, tattling habit is accompanied with a malicious disposition; and then, look out for mischief. It was of such a one that Solomon was speaking, when he said, "A whisperer separateth chief friends."

Mary and Nancy Worthley had two cousins, Jane

and Eliza Mason, who lived very near, and with whom they were very intimate. They loved each other as much as if they had been sisters. After some time, however, Mrs. Worthley observed that Mary did not seem so glad as usual when Jane and Eliza came to see her; and she did not so often ask leave to go and visit them. Even little Nancy's eyes did not now sparkle as they used to, at the thought of going to Col. Mason's.

One afternoon, Mrs. Worthley went away, and left Mary to entertain a company of her young friends. Among these were her two cousins. When Mrs. Worthley returned home, the company were gone, and Mary and Nancy appeared vexed and unhappy. "O mother," said Mary, "I wish Jane and Eliza would never come here again, and that you would never send me to their house." "What! my love, your dear cousins?" "I don't want to call them cousins any more. They have spoiled our visit this afternoon." "What have they done, my daughter?" "Why, we talked about some old affairs, and Sarah Porter and I told them how naughty they had been; but they said it was not so, and were displeased, and cried about it, and made us all unhappy."

"But what are the old affairs, that make them such naughty girls?" inquired Mrs. Worthley. "You do not tell me what wicked things your cousins have done."

"O mother, they have not loved me this good while, because I was a better scholar at school than they; so they would go and tell tales about me to their mother and all the girls. They always laugh, too, about my dress, and make game of my looks and words. When they come here, it is only to get something to talk about, and to make themselves merry with. I am sure I never shall go to their house any more; and Sarah and Dolly Porter shall be my cousins."

"But, my daughter, how do you know that your cousins have been so wicked? Have you ever seen any such actions in them yourself?"

"O, no; they are very kind to my face, and profess as much friendship as ever; but that only shows that they are artful, and put on a fair show to deceive me the easier."

"How, then, do you know?"

"O, Sarah Porter has told me about it a great many times. She has been so kind as to watch their conduct towards me, and let me know about it, or I might never have found it out."

"Could not any of the other girls in the neighbourhood have told you? Have they not seen some of these misdeeds?"

(*Hesitatingly.*) "I do not know that any of them have."

"Have none of them ever spoken to you about it? Has not Dolly Porter confirmed her sister's story?"

"No, ma'am."

"What, then, did all the girls say, when you told your cousins of their wickedness so plainly?"

"At first, we didn't let them hear what we said to Eliza and Jane. But they found out something was the matter; and when we told them, they would not believe a word of it."

"So, then, nobody knew any thing against them but you and Sarah."

"Nobody but Sarah. I know nothing but what she has told me."

"But how could you and Sarah maintain your ground against the whole company, and against the two girls, who protested that they were innocent?'

"I don't know, only that Sarah talked very fast and loud, and kept all in confusion till they went away."

"I am sorry to say, my daughter, that Sarah Porter has accused your cousins falsely, and that you have been duped by her stories, till you have treated your best friends very ill indeed. Your suspicions of Eliza and Jane must be groundless. If they had long done as Sarah says, you would have seen it yourself, and I should have noticed it long ago; and so would the rest of your play-mates. But it seems that every body has been blind and deaf except the *dear and friendly* Miss Sarah. Not even her own sister will believe that your cousins are guilty. All this looks very much as if *Sarah* was the guilty one, and had made up false reports, to do mischief. I will tell you, Mary, what I have seen. I have observed that you did not treat your cousins so kindly as you had done, and that they appeared grieved and distant, of course; while I have had no suspicion of their being envious or disposed to talk against you. I have seen, also, that Sarah Porter is apt to talk about other people, and I have feared that she indulged in idle gossip and tale-bearing."

"O I see it now, mother. This is the work of poor Sarah, alone. She told some things first *as a great secret*, that made me suspicious of my cousins, and ready to listen to her again. Since that time, when I have seen her, she has done nothing but *whisper, whisper, whisper* about Eliza and Jane, till she has made me believe almost any thing. I have not a doubt they are innocent. I will go to them in the morning, confess the injury I have done them, and beg them to forgive me."

"This story illustrates the Proverb of Solomon, "A whisperer separateth chief friends." Sarah Porter was a whisperer, and she separated these little friends, who loved each other as sisters. A whisperer is a very bad character. If you will read the 29th, 30th, and 31st verses of the first chapter of Romans, you will see that Paul classes them with the very vilest of characters.

CHAPTER XXV.

THERE is, perhaps, no accomplishment which will add so much to your character and influence, as the art of conversing agreeably and well. To do this, however, requires a cultivated mind, richly stored with a variety of useful information; a good taste, a delicate sense of propriety; a good use of language; and an easy and fluent expression.

The most of these requisites can be acquired; and the rest, if naturally deficient, can be greatly improved. An easy, fluent expression is sometimes a natural talent; but, when not joined with a good understanding and a cultivated mind, it degenerates into mere loquacity. But, in order to be prepared to converse well, you must not only have your mind *well stored*, but its contents, if I may so speak, *well arranged;* so that you can at any time call forth its resources, upon any subject, when they are needed.

One of the principal difficulties in the way of conversing well, is a hesitancy of speech, a difficulty of expressing one's ideas with ease and grace. This may arise from various causes. It may proceed from affectation, a desire to speak in fine, showy style. This will invariably defeat its object. You can never appear, in the eyes of intelligent and well-bred people, to be what you are not. The more simple and unaffected your style is, provided it be pure and chaste, the better you will appear. Affectation will only make you ridiculous. But the same difficulty may arise from diffidence, which leads to embarrassment; and embarrassment clouds the memory, and produces confusion of mind and hesitancy of speech. This must be overcome by degrees, by cultivating self-possession, and frequenting good society. The same difficulty may, likewise, arise from the want of a sufficient command of language to express one's ideas with ease and fluency. This is to be obtained by writing; by reading the most pure and classic authors, such as Addison's Spectator; and by observing the conversation of well-educated people. In order to have a good supply of well-chosen words at ready command, Mr. Whelpley recommends selecting from a dictionary several hundred words, such as are in most common use, and required especially in ordinary conversation, writing them down, and committing them to memory, so as to have them as familiar as the letters of the alphabet. A professional gentleman informs me, that he has overcome this difficulty by reading a well-written story till it becomes trite and uninteresting, and then frequently reading it aloud, without any regard to the story, but only to the language, in order to accustom the organs of speech to an easy flow of words. I have no doubt that such experiments as these would be successful in giving a freedom and ease of expression, which is often greatly impeded for want of just the word that is needed at a given time.

There is no species of information but may be available to improve and enrich the conversation, and make it interesting to the various classes of people. As an example of this, a clergyman recently informed me that a rich man, who is engaged extensively in the iron business, but who is very irreligious, put up with him for the night. The minister, knowing the character of his guest, directed his conversation to those subjects in which he supposed him to be chiefly interested. He exhibited specimens of iron ore, of which he possessed a variety; explained their different qualities; spoke of the various modes of manufacturing it, and explained the process of manufacturing steel, interspersing his conversation with occasional serious reflections on the wisdom and goodness of God, in providing so abundantly the metals most necessary for the common purposes of life, and thus leading the man's mind "from Nature up to Nature's God." The man entered readily into the conversation, appeared deeply interested, and afterwards expressed his great admiration of the minister. The man was prejudiced against ministers. This conversation may so far remove his prejudices as to open his ear to the truth. But all this the minister was enabled to do, by acquainting himself with a branch of knowledge which many would suppose to be of no use to a minister. By conversing freely with all sorts of people upon that which chiefly interests them, you may not only secure their good-will, but greatly increase your own stock of knowledge. There is no one so ignorant but he may, in this way, add something to your general information; and you may improve the opportunity it gives to impart useful information, without seeming to do it.

RULES FOR CONVERSATION.

I. AVOID *affectation*. Instead of making you appear to better advantage, it will only expose you to ridicule.

II. Avoid *low expressions.* There is a dialect peculiar to low people, which you cannot imitate without appearing as if you were yourself low-bred.

III. Avoid *provincialisms.* There are certain expressions peculiar to particular sections of the country. For example, in New England, many people are in the habit of interlarding their conversation with the phrase, "*You see.*" In Pennsylvania and New York, the same use is made of "*You know.*" And in the West and South, phrases peculiar to those sections of the country are still more common and ludicrous. Avoid all these expressions, and strive after a pure, chaste, and simple style.

IV. Avoid all *ungrammatical* expressions.

V. Avoid *unmeaning exclamations,* as, "O my!" "O mercy!" and such like.

VI. Never speak unless you have *something to say.* "A word fitly spoken is like apples of gold in pictures of silver."

VII. Avoid *prolixity.* Make your language concise and perspicuous, and strive not to prolong your speech beyond what is necessary, remembering that others wish to speak as well as yourself. Be sparing of anecdote; and only resort to it when you have a good illustration of some subject before the company, or when you have a piece of information of general interest. To tell a story well, is a great art. To be tedious and prolix in story-telling, is insufferable. To avoid this, do not attempt to relate every minute particular, but seize upon the grand points. Take the following specimen of the relation of the same incident by two different persons: "You see, I got up this morning, and dressed myself, and came down stairs, and opened the front door; and O, if it didn't look beautiful! For, you see, the sun shone on the dew, the dew, you know, that hangs in great drops on the grass in the morning. Well, as the sun shone on the dew drops, it was all sparkling, like so many diamonds; and it looked so inviting, you see, I thought I must have a walk. So, you see, I went out into the street, and got over the fence; the fence, you know, the back side of the barn. Well, I got over it, and walked into the grove, and there I heard the blue jay, and cock-robin, and ever so many pretty birds, singing so sweetly. I went along the foot-path to a place where there is a stump; the great stump, you know, James, by the side of the path. Well, there, O my! what should I see, but a grey squirrel running up a tree!"

How much better the following: "Early this morning, just as the sun was peeping over the hill, and the green grass was all over sparkling with diamonds, as the sun shone upon the dew drops, I had a delightful walk in the grove, listening to the sweet music of the birds, and watching the motions of a beautiful grey squirrel, running up a tree, and hopping nimbly from branch to branch." Here is the story, better told, in less than half the words.

Never specify any particulars which would readily be understood without. In the relation of this inci-dent, all the circumstances detailed in the first specimen, previous to entering the grove, are super-fluous; for if you were in the grove early in the morning, you could not get there without getting out of your bed, dressing yourself, opening the door, going into the street, and getting over the fence. The moment you speak of being in the grove early in the morning, the mind of the hearer supplies all these preliminaries; and your specifying them only excites his impatience to get at the point of your story. Be careful, also, that you never relate the same anecdote the second time to the same company; neither set up a laugh at your own story.

VIII. Never interrupt others while they are speaking. Quietly wait till they have finished what they have to say, before you reply. To interrupt others in conversation is very unmannerly.

IX. You will sometimes meet with very talkative persons, who are not disposed to give you a fair chance. *Let them talk on.* They will be better pleased, and you will save your words and your feelings.

X. Avoid, as much as possible, *speaking of yourself.* When we meet a person who is always saying *I,* telling what he has done, and how he does things, the impression it gives us of him is unpleasant. We say, "He thinks he knows every thing and can teach every body. He is great in his own eyes. He thinks more of himself than of every body else." True politeness leads us to keep ourselves out of view, and show an interest in other people's affairs.

XI. Endeavour to make your conversation *useful.* Introduce some subject which will be profitable to the company you are in. You feel dissatisfied when you retire from company where nothing useful has been said. But there is no amusement more interesting, to a sensible person, than intelligent conversation upon elevated subjects. It leaves a happy impression upon the mind. You can retire from it, and lay your head upon your pillow with a quiet conscience.

Illustrations.

FEMALE INFLUENCE.

THERE are some things, which females can do, in a modest, quiet way, to exert a good influence upon others, to much better effect than the other sex. Perhaps there is nothing in which they can do this more effectively than in checking such evil habits as drinking intoxicating liquors, using tobacco and an indulgence in impiety, vulgarity, and profaneness of speech.

Their persuasive appeals, or keen rebukes, will often be received, when, if they came from a man, they would only give offence, and excite anger.

SWEARING IN HEBREW.

A YOUNG lady in the cars was very much annoyed by the conversation of a young naval officer, which was intermingled with oaths. After bearing it a while, and seeing no improvement, she inquired, "Sir, can you converse in the Hebrew tongue?" He replied that he could, expecting, no doubt, to have the pleasure of holding some learned conversation with her. She then very politely told him that, if he wished to swear any more, he would greatly oblige herself, and probably the rest of the passengers, if he would swear in that language. The young man was silent the rest of the way. Profaneness, besides being an impious offence against God, is universally considered as too *vulgar* to be indulged in the presence of ladies. It is such an offence against decency and propriety, that, in any company, they will be sustained in rebuking it. But it has a much finer effect, when it can be done in such a style as this. Probably the young man never will forget it as long as he lives.

THE SEA CAPTAIN.

A YOUNG gentleman was standing with a young lady on the deck of a steamboat, conversing on the comparative beauty of a storm and a calm at sea, when suddenly they had the opportunity of making the comparison. The heavens became black as night. The wind moaned through the ship's rigging. The thunder came nearer, and the lightning wreathed the clouds with its flame. The black waters foamed angrily, and the waves went rolling and tumbling onward, dashing their crested tops to the clouds, while the boat was tossing like a feather in the wind, now mounting on the billow, and now sinking again to the depths. There was hurrying to and fro upon the deck, and anxiety on many a countenance. The loud shout of the commander was heard above the voice of the tempest, issuing orders to the crew. He came near where the young gentleman and lady were standing and awoke them from their reverie of admiration, by a blast from his speaking-trumpet, giving some command to his men. The command not being obeyed, it was repeated, accompanied with horrid oaths and curses.

The young lady started, and, with a shudder, said to her companion, "I fear not the voice of the tempest, or the wrath of the deep, or the fiery footsteps of Jehovah, as he walks upon the wings of the whirlwind; but I dare not stand in the presence of a man who curses his God.   Let us go below."

As they passed away, the captain turned and looked upon them, with an air which told that he heard and felt the remark.   After the storm had passed away, the captain sought the lady, and begged her pardon, promising never again to take the name of God in vain.   With expressions of gratitude to God, she drew a small Bible from her side, and presented it to him, saying, she hoped it might work in him a greater and holier reformation.

Some years after, this young lady with her father and mother were at church, in a strange city, listening to the burning eloquence of a man, whose whole soul was absorbed in the mighty theme of the Cross. When he came down from the pulpit, he greeted the strangers, and, lifting a small volume towards heaven, expressed his gratitude at beholding again the person who had given him that Bible, with that kind admonition, through which the blasphemous sea captain was changed to a minister of righteousness.

CHAPTER XXVI.

INQUISITIVENESS.

THE inhabitants of New England have the reputation of being inquisitive to a fault; and perhaps with some justice. This disposition grows out of a good trait of character, carried to an extreme. It comes from a desire after knowledge. But this desire becomes excessive, when exercised with reference to matters which it does not concern us to know. When it leads us to pry into the concerns of others, from a mere vain curiosity, it becomes a vice. There are some people who can never be satisfied, till they *see the inside of every thing*. They must know the why and the wherefore of every thing they meet with. I have heard an amusing anecdote of this sort. There was a man who had lost his nose. A *Yankee*, seeing him, desired to know how so strange a thing had happened. After enduring his importunity for some time, the man declared he would tell him, if he would promise to ask him no more questions; to which the other agreed. "Well," said the man, "*it was bit off*." "Ah," replied the Yankee, "*I wish I knew who bit it off!*" This is a fair specimen of the morbid appetite created by excessive inquisitiveness.

When inquisitiveness goes no farther than a strong

desire to obtain useful information, and to inquire into the reason of things, or when it desires information concerning the affairs of others from benevolent sympathy, then it is a valuable trait of character. But when the object is to gratify an idle curiosity, it is annoying to others, and often leads the person who indulges it into serious difficulty. And the more it is indulged, the more it craves. If you gratify this disposition till it grows into a habit, you will find it very difficult to control. You will never be able to let any thing alone. You will want to look into every drawer in the house; to open every bundle that you see; and never be satisfied till you have seen the inside of every thing. This will lead you into temptation. It can hardly be supposed that one who is so anxious to *see* every thing should have no desire to *possess* the things that are seen. Thus, what began in curiosity may end in coveting and thieving. But if it does not lead you so far astray as this, it will bring you into serious difficulty with your parents, or your friends, whose guest you are; for they will not be satisfied to have their drawers tumbled, packages opened, and every nice article fingered. This disposition, too, will lead you to inquire into the secrets of your friends; and this will furnish a temptation to tattling. What you have been at such pains to obtain, you will find it difficult to keep to yourself. You will want to share the rare enjoyment with others. And when the story comes round to your friend or companion, whose confidence you have betrayed, you will, to your great chagrin and mortification, be discarded. A delicate sense of propriety will lead you to avoid prying too closely into the affairs of others. You will never do it from mere curiosity. But if any of your friends so far make you a confident as to lead you to suppose that they need your sympathy or aid, you may, in a delicate manner, inquire further, in order to ascertain what aid you can render. You may, also, make some general inquiries of strangers, in order to show an interest in their affairs. But beyond this, you cannot safely indulge this disposition.

CHAPTER XXVII.

IT often requires great courage to say NO. But by being able promptly, on occasion, to utter this little monosyllable, you may save yourself a deal of trouble. If mother Eve had known how to say *no*, she might have saved herself and her posterity from ruin. And many of her children, who have lost their character and their all, might have been saved, if they had only had courage promptly to say NO. Your safety and happiness depend upon it.

You are importuned by some of your companions to engage in some amusement, or to go on some excursion, which you know to be wrong. You resolutely and promptly say *No* at the outset, and there is the end of it. But if you hesitate, you will be urged and importuned, until you will probably yield; and having thus given up your own judgment, and violated your conscience, you will lose your power of resistance, and yield to every enticement.

Jane has cultivated decision of character. She never hesitates a moment, when any thing wrong is proposed. She rejects it instantly. The consequence is, her companions never think of coming to her, with any proposal of a questionable nature. Her prompt and

decisive NO they do not desire to encounter. Her
parents can trust her any where, because they have no
fears of her being led astray. And this relieves them
of a load of anxiety.

But Mary is the opposite of this. She wants to
please every body, and therefore has not courage to
say *no* to any. She seems to have no power to resist
temptation. Hence, she is always getting into difficulty, always doing something that she ought not, or
going to some improper place, or engaging in some
improper diversions, through the enticement of her
companions. Her parents scarcely dare trust her out
of their sight, they are so fearful that she will be led
astray. She is a source of great anxiety to them; and
all because she cannot say NO.

Now, let me beg of you to learn to say NO. If
you find any difficulty in uttering it, if your tongue
won't do its office, or if you find a *"frog in your
throat,"* which obstructs your utterance, go by yourself, and practise *saying* No, NO, NO! till you can
articulate clearly, distinctly, and without hesitation;
and have it always ready on your tongue's end, to
utter with emphasis to every girl or boy, man or
woman, or evil spirit, that presumes to propose to you
to do any thing that is wrong. Only be careful to
say it respectfully and courteously, with the usual
prefixes and *suffixes,* which properly belong to the persons to whom you are speaking.

CHAPTER XXVIII.

CAN you find any thing, in all the works of Nature, which is not made for some use? The cow gives milk, the ox labours in the field, the sheep furnishes wool for clothing, and all of them provide us with meat. The horse and the dog are the servants of man. Every animal, every little insect, has its place, and its work to perform, carrying out the great design of its Creator. And so it is with the inanimate creation. The earth yields its products for the use of man and beast; and the sun, and the air, and the clouds, (each in turn,) help forward the work. And to how many thousand uses do we put the noble, stately tree! It furnishes houses for us to live in, furniture for our convenience, fuel to make us warm, ships to sail in, and to bring us the productions of other lands. It yields us fruit for food, and to gratify our taste. And so you may go through all the variety of animal and vegetable life, and you will find every thing designed for some use. And, though there may be some things of the use of which you are ignorant, yet you will find every thing made with such evidence of design, that you cannot help thinking it must have been intended for some use.

Now, if every thing in creation is designed for some use, surely you ought not to think of being useless, or of living for nothing. God made you to be useful; and, to answer the end of your being, you must begin early to learn to be useful. "But how can I be useful?" you may ask. "I wish to be useful. I am anxious to be qualified to fill some useful station in life, to be a missionary or a teacher, or in some other way to do good. But I do not see what good I can do now." Though you may not say this in so many words, yet I have no doubt that such thoughts may often have passed through your mind. Many people long to be useful, as they suppose, but think they must be in some other situation, to afford them the opportunity. This is a great mistake. God, who made all creatures, has put every one in the right place. In the place where God has put you, there you may find some useful thing to do. Do you ask me what useful thing you can do? You may find a hundred opportunities for doing good, and being useful, every day, if you watch for them. You can be useful in assisting your mother; you can be useful in helping your brothers and sisters; you can be useful in school, by supporting the authority of your teacher, and by being kind and helpful to your playmates. If you make it the great aim of your life to be useful, you will never lack opportunities.

I have seen young persons, who would take great delight in mere play or amusement; but the moment they were directed to do any thing useful, they would be displeased. Now, I do not object to amusement in its proper place; for a suitable degree of amusement is useful to the health. But pleasure alone, is a small object to live for; and if you attempt to live only to be amused, you will soon run the whole round of pleasure, and become tired of it all. But if you make it your great object to be useful, and seek your chief pleasure therein, you will engage in occasional amusement with a double relish. No one can be happy who is not useful. Pleasure soon satiates. One amusement soon *grows grey*, and another is sought, till, at length, they all become tasteless and insipid.

Let it be your object, then, every day of your life, to be useful to yourself and others. In the morning, ask yourself, "What useful things can I do to-day? What can I do that will be a lasting benefit to myself? How can I make myself useful in the family? What can I do for my father or mother? What for my brothers or sisters? And what disinterested act can I perform for the benefit of those who have no claim upon me?" Thus you will cultivate useful habits and benevolent feelings. And you will find a rich return into your own bosom. By making yourself useful to every body, you will find every one making a return of your kindness. You will secure their friendship and good will, as well as their bounty. You will find it, then, both for your interest and happiness to BE USEFUL.

Illustrations.

BENEVOLENCE.

On her death bed, a pious widow in England called her daughter, and said to her, "Here are twenty pounds: I wish you, after my death, to give this money to the missionary cause; and, depend upon it, you will never have any reason to be sorry for having given it." This was when the missionary cause first began to attract attention in England, and when many people ridiculed it. But the daughter cheerfully obeyed the dying command of her mother, though little expecting ever in any way to meet a return. But she had a son who became exceedingly profligate, and brought heart-rending trouble upon his mother. He became utterly unmanageable, either by tenderness or authority, and at length forsook his friends, entered the army, and vanished from their knowledge. The Providence of God led him to India. There he fell in company with a Christian missionary, who dealt faithfully with him, and was the means of his conversion to God. After a while, the young man himself became a missionary, and wrote to his mother, imploring her forgiveness, and informing her of the alteration that had taken place in him, and in his employment. Here was her mother's gift returned into her bosom a hundred-fold. But the Lord repays bountifully those who lend to him. This woman had a second son, who was likewise a profligate, and had entered the army before this news reached her. He also was led to India. There he was taken sick; and, being affectionately attended by the missionaries, he also was brought to repentance. His eldest brother, who was several hundred miles distant, and who did not know that he was in India, was providentially led to visit the station at this time. On hearing from the missionaries the interesting facts in the case, he visited the young man, and, to his great surprise and joy, discovered in the sick youth his own brother! He remained with him till his death, which was peaceful and happy. This narrative shows that *it is profitable to give to the Lord,* and illustrates the proverb, " Cast thy bread upon the waters, and thou shalt find it after many days."

A LESSON FROM THE BIRDS.

A Gentleman observed, in a thicket of bushes near his dwelling, a collection of brown thrushes, who, for several days, attracted his attention by their loud cries and strange movements. At length, his curiosity was so much excited, that he determined to see if he could ascertain the cause of the excitement among them. On examining the bushes, he found a female thrush, whose wing was caught in a limb in such a way, that she could not escape. Near by was her nest, containing several half-grown birds. On retiring a little distance, a company of thrushes appeared, with worms and other insects in their mouths, which they gave first to the mother, and then to her young; she, the meanwhile, cheering them on in their labour of love, with a song of gratitude. After watching the interesting scene till his curiosity was satisfied, the gentleman released the poor bird, when she flew to her nest with a grateful song to her deliverer; and her charitable neighbours dispersed to their several abodes, singing, as they went, a song of joy.

"Isn't that beautiful?" exclaims a sweet little girl, whose happy face and joyous song, and golden ringlets waving in the air, remind one of the merry songsters of the grove. Beautiful! Indeed, it is. But I can tell you what is more beautiful still. It is that little girl who drops sweet words, kind remarks, and pleasant smiles, as she passes along; who has a kind word of sympathy for every girl or boy she meets in trouble, and a kind hand to help her companions out of difficulty; who never scowls, never contends, never teazes her mates, nor seeks in any other way to diminish, but always to increase their happiness. Would it not please you to pick up a string of pearls, drops of gold, diamonds, and precious stones, as you pass along the streets? But these are the true pearls and precious stones, which can never be lost. Take the hand of the friendless. Smile on the sad and dejected. Sympathize with those in trouble. Strive every where to diffuse around you sunshine and joy.

If you do this, you will be sure to be beloved. Dr. Doddridge one day asked his little girl why it was that every body loved her. "I know not," she replied, "unless it be that I love every body." This is the true secret of being beloved. "He that hath friends,' says Solomon, "must show himself friendly." Love begets love. If you love others, they cannot help loving you. So, then, do not put on a scowl, and fretfully complain that nobody loves you, or that such or such a one does not like you. If nobody loves you, it is your own fault. Either you do not make yourself lovely by a sweet temper and kind winning ways, or you do not love those of whom you complain.

MISS RACHEL COWIE; AFTERWARDS WIFE OF REV. DR. MILNE, MISSIONARY TO CHINA.

THE following brief memoir shows the importance of a knowledge of some useful employment, even to females in high life. It likewise exhibits a beautiful picture of filial piety, diligence, and prudence.

Miss Cowie's father was a wealthy man, engaged in extensive business. He lived in Aberdeen, Scotland. But, in that country, the females of many families in the higher ranks of society, as well as those in middling circumstances, are instructed in some branch of business suited to their ability. This is an excellent custom; for, whatever may be our circumstances to-day, we know not what they will be to-morrow. Riches are no sure dependence, for they often " take to themselves wings." This is especially the case in this country, where reverses are so common. That your father is rich to-day is no evidence that he will be so a few years hence. It is therefore necessary that you should be prepared to provide for yourself; and, to be so, you must not despise any employment that is useful and suitable for your sex.

Rachel Cowie was early put to learn a branch of the millinery business; which she industriously acquired, though she knew not that she should ever need it. But, after a while, her father's business began to decline, and at length he failed. He gave up to his creditors every thing but their wearing apparel and a few books. Both her parents were infirm, with no means of support in their old age. There was no one but herself on whom they could depend. When Rachel saw the decline of her father's business, she obtained his consent to set up her own. She had a small sum of money, and she borrowed a little more of a friend to begin with. She began her business, praying that God would prosper it, and keep her from the new temptations to which she should be exposed. She was successful. In a few months, she was able to pay what she had borrowed, and to furnish a house for herself.

When her father's business completely failed, and her parents were thrown upon the world, destitute of the means of support, she was prepared to receive them into her own house. She supported them by her labours; nursed them with the utmost tenderness in their illness; attended them in their last sickness, and saw them die in the hope of glory. While they lived, she would listen to no proposals of marriage; but, after their death, she became the wife of Rev. Dr. Milne, and accompanied him on his mission to China, where she was a great solace and comfort to him, and a helper to him in his labours.

Learn not to despise any useful employment; but deem it honourable to be able to provide for yourself, and to help others.

3   R

CHAPTER XXIX.

ON BEING CONTENTED.

GODLINESS, says the apostle Paul, *"with* CON-
TENTMENT, is great gain." These two are *great
gain,* because, without them, all the gain in the
world will not make us happy. Young people are apt
to think, if they had this thing or that, or if they were
in such and such circumstances, different from their
own, they would be happy. Sometimes they think, if
their parents were only rich, they should enjoy themselves. But rich people are often more anxious to increase their riches than poor people are to be rich;
and the more their artificial wants are gratified, the
more they are increased. "The eye is not satisfied
with seeing, nor the ear filled with hearing." Solomon
was a great king, so rich that he was able to get whatever his heart desired. He built great palaces for
himself; he filled them with servants; he treasured up
gold and silver; he bought gardens, and vineyards, and
fields; he bought herds of cattle, with horses and
carriages; he kept men and women singers, and players
on all sorts of instruments; whatever his eyes desired
he kept not from them; he withheld not his heart
from any joy; but with it all he was not satisfied. He
called it all "vanity and vexation of spirit." So you
may set your heart at rest, that riches will not make
you happy. Nor would you be any more happy, if

you could exchange places with some other persons, who seem to you to have many more means of enjoyment than yourself. With these things that dazzle your eyes, they have also their trials; and if you take their place, you must take the bitter with the sweet.

But young people sometimes think, if they were only men and women, and could manage for themselves, and have none to control them, then they would certainly be happy, for they could do as they please. But in this they are greatly mistaken. There will then be a great increase of care and labour; and they will find it more difficult to *do as they please* than they do now. If they have none to control them, they will have none to provide for them. True, they may then manage for themselves; but they will also have to support themselves. Those who have lived the longest, generally consider youth the happiest period of life, because it is comparatively free from trouble and care, and there is more time for pleasure and amusement.

But there is one lesson, which, if you will learn it in youth, will make you happy all your days. It is the lesson which Paul had learned. You know that he suffered great hardships in travelling on foot, in various countries, to preach the Gospel. He was often persecuted, reviled, defamed, beaten, and imprisoned. Yet he says, *"I have learned in whatsoever state I am, therewith to be content."* There are several things which should teach us this lesson. In the first place, God, in his holy providence, has placed us in the condition where we are. He knows what is best for us, and what will best serve the end for which he made us; and of all other situations, he has chosen for us the one that we now occupy. Who could choose so well as he? And then, what can we gain by fretting about it, and worrying ourselves for what we cannot help? We only make ourselves unhappy. Morever, it is very ungrateful and wicked to complain of our lot, since God has given us more and better than we deserve. It is better to look about us, and see how many things we have to be thankful for; to look upon *what we have*, rather than *what we have not*. This does not, indeed, forbid our seeking to improve our condition, provided we do it with submission to the will of God. We ought to use all fair and lawful means to this end; but not in such a spirit of discontent and repining, as will make us miserable if we are disappointed. If you desire to be happy, then, BE CONTENTED.

CHAPTER XXX.

UNION OF SERIOUS PIETY WITH HABITUAL CHEERFULNESS.

IT is a mistake often made by young people, to associate religion with a downcast look, a sad countenance, and an aching heart. Perhaps the mistakes of some good people, in putting on a grave and severe aspect, approaching even to moroseness, may have given some occasion for this sentiment. I do not know, indeed, how prevalent the sentiment is among the young. I can hardly think it is common with those who are religiously educated. As for myself, I well remember that, in my childhood, I thought true Christians must be the happiest people in the world. There is no doubt, however, that many pleasure-loving young people do look upon religion with that peculiar kind of dread which they feel of the presence of a grave severe maiden aunt, which would spoil all their pleasure. And I do not deny, that there are certain kinds of pleasure which religion spoils; but then it first removes the taste and desire for them, after which the spoliation is nothing to be lamented. It is true, also, that there are some things in religion which are painful. Repentance for sin is a painful exercise; self-denial is painful; the resistance of temptation is sometimes trying; and the subduing of evil dispositions is a difficult work. But to endure whatever of suffering there is in these things, is a saving in the end. It is less painful than the tortures of a guilty conscience, the gnawings of remorse, and the fear of hell. It is easier to be endured than the consequences of neglecting religion. If you get a sliver in your finger, it is easier to bear the pain of having it removed, than it is to carry it about with you. If you have a decayed tooth, it is easier to have it extracted than to bear the toothache. So it is easier to repent of sin than to bear remorse and fear. And the labour of resisting temptation, and of restraining and subduing evil dispositions, is not so great an interference with one's happiness as it is to carry about a guilty conscience.

There is, however, nothing in true piety inconsistent with habitual cheerfulness. There is a difference between cheerfulness and levity. Cheerfulness is serene and peaceful. Levity is light and trifling. The former promotes evenness of temper and equanimity of enjoyment; the latter drowns sorrow and pain for a short time, only to have it return again with redoubled power.

The Christian hope, and the promises and consolations of God's word, furnish the only true ground of cheerfulness. Who should be cheerful and happy, if not one who is delivered from the terrors of hell and the fear of death, who is raised to the dignity of a child of God, who has the hope of eternal life, the prospect of dwelling for ever in the presence of God, in the society of the blessed, and in the enjoyment of perfect felicity? But no one would associate these things with that peculiar kind of mirth, which is the delight of the pleasure-loving world. Your sense of propriety recoils from the idea of associating things of such high import with rudeness, frolicking, and mirth. Yet there is an innocent gayety of spirits, arising from natural vivacity, especially in the period of childhood and youth, the indulgence of which, within proper bounds, religion does not forbid.

There is a happy medium between a settled, severe gravity and gloom, and frivolity, levity, and mirth, which young Christians should strive to cultivate. If you give unbounded licence to a mirthful spirit, and indulge freely in all manner of levity, frivolity, and foolish jesting, you cannot maintain that devout state of heart which is essential to true piety. On the other hand, if you studiously repress the natural vivacity of youthful feeling, and cultivate a romantic kind of melancholy, or a severe gravity, you will destroy the elasticity of your spirits, injure your health, and very likely become peevish and irritable, and of a sour, morose temper; and this will be quite as injurious to true religious feeling as the other. The true medium is, to unite serious piety with habitual cheerfulness. Always bring Christian motives to bear upon your feelings. The Gospel of Jesus Christ has a remedy for every thing in life that is calculated to make us gloomy and sad. It offers the pardon of sin to the penitent and believing, the aid of grace to those that struggle against an evil disposition, and succour and help against temptation. It promises to relieve the believer from fear, and afford consolation in affliction.

There is no reason why a true Christian should not be cheerful. There are, indeed, many things, which he sees, within and without, that must give him pain. But there is that in his Christian hope, and in the considerations brought to his mind from the Word of God, which is able to bear him high above them all.

Let me, then, earnestly recommend you to cultivate

a serious but cheerful piety. Let your religion be neither of that spurious kind which expends itself in sighs, and tears, and gloomy feelings, nor that which makes you insensible to all feeling. But while you are alive to your own sins and imperfections, exercising godly sorrow for them, and while you feel a deep and earnest sympathy for those who have no interest in Christ, let your faith in the atoning blood of Jesus, and your confidence in God, avail to keep you from sinking into melancholy and gloom, and make you cheerful and happy, while you rest in God.

Farewell.

And now, gentle reader, after this long conversation, I must take leave of you, commending you to God, with the prayer that my book may be useful to you, in the formation of a well-balanced Christian character; and that, after you and I shall have done the errand for which the Lord sent us into the world, we may meet in heaven. GOD BLESS YOU!

WILLIAM COLLINS & CO., PRINTERS.